CLASSICAL DANCE AND THEATRE IN SOUTH-EAST ASIA

CLASSICAL DANCE AND THEATRE IN SOUTH-EAST ASIA

Jukka O. Miettinen

Singapore
OXFORD UNIVERSITY PRESS
Oxford New York
1992

Oxford University Press, Walton Street, Oxford OX2 6DP

Oxford New York Toronto
Delhi Bombay Calcutta Madras Karachi
Kuala Lumpur Singapore Hong Kong Tokyo
Nairobi Dar es Salaam Cape Town
Melbourne Auckland Madrid
and associated companies in
Berlin Ibadan

Oxford is a trade mark of Oxford University Press

Published in the United States
by Oxford University Press, New York

British Library Cataloguing in Publication Data
Data available

Library of Congress Cataloging-in-Publication Data

Miettinen, Jukka O.
  Classical dance and theatre in South-East Asia/
Jukka O. Miettinen.
    p. cm.
  Includes bibliographical references and index.
  ISBN 0-19-588595-3
  1. Theater—Asia, Southeastern. 2. Puppet theater—Asia,
Southeastern. 3. Dancing—Asia, Southeastern. I. Title.
PN2860.M538 1992
792'.0959—dc20
92–10946
CIP

Typeset by Typeset Gallery Sdn. Bhd., Malaysia
Printed in Singapore by Kyodo Printing Co. (S) Pte. Ltd.
Published by Oxford University Press Pte. Ltd.,
Unit 221, Ubi Avenue 4, Singapore 1440

Acknowledgements

MUCH has been written about theatre and dance in Asia, especially India and Japan, but surprisingly little has been published on the South-East Asian traditions, which led to this attempt to gather together the scattered information into a comprehensive book on this subject.

Years of travel and work in South-East Asia have given me the opportunity to become acquainted with its rich theatrical traditions. In this I received much encouragement in the early 1980s from Dr Upraity, the head of the cultural section and my superior at Unesco in Bangkok, and Ms Suchitra Vuthisathira, the former head of the SEAMEO Project in Archaeology and Fine Arts (SPAFA), for which I am most grateful. I am also very obliged to the Fine Arts Department of Thailand for the opportunity to see and document performances. I am much indebted to the excellent *Theatre in Southeast Asia*, now an approved classic, which was written in the 1960s by Professor James R. Brandon. Although much of my book relies on the work of others, and readers familiar with the subject may easily recognize many of its sources, listed in the Bibliography, I have also received invaluable information from specialists, among whom I especially wish to mention Dr Surapone Virulak of Chulalongkorn University, Bangkok and Dr Soedarsono from Institut Seni Indonesia (ISI) in Yogyakarta. The responsibility for any errors, however, is mine alone. Whilst these sources proved more than fruitful, my work was naturally restricted by the political situation in the 1980s, a period when some of the South-East Asian countries have been more or less closed to outsiders.

During the final period of work in Finland, my native country, I was assisted by many institutes and private photographers who have generously allowed me to use their material. The details are given in the captions. As I usually write in Finnish, I needed assistance in preparing the present manuscript and I have been patiently helped by Jüri Kokkonen, Raimo Kaipainen, Jane O'Neill, and Fredrik Lagus. Special thanks must go to Ari Tenhula, my friend, and himself a dancer, who not only encouraged my work but also gave the initial impulse for it.

Finally, I would like to pay tribute to one specific group of artists, without whom this work would never have been possible—the countless actors and dancers, who often anonymously (as unfortunately is mostly the case on these pages as well) maintain the magnificent theatrical traditions of South-East Asia. It is to them that I would like to dedicate this book.

Helsinki   JUKKA O. MIETTINEN
30 November 1991

Contents

Colour Plates

Between pages 108 and 109.

Plates

Figures

Introduction

THE lustrous, cool beauty of the *khon* mask theatre of Thailand, the puppet-like movements of Burmese dancers, and the soft, meditative elegance of the *wayang wong* dance-drama of Java are all superb expressions of the classical performing arts in South-East Asia. The theatrical traditions of South-East Asia can be compared in their grandeur and degree of stylization with other great theatre genres developed over many centuries, such as European opera and ballet, or the *kabuki* of Japan and the *kathakali* of India. Each of them has its own well-known stories, refined music, aesthetics, and unique techniques of representation.

A theatre genre crystallized in classical form is an extremely sensitive and complex whole. It requires the close co-operation of specialists of many forms of art and an unbroken tradition extending over generations. It reflects necessarily the history and ideals of the culture that created it. Theatre has often been called living history, and in South-East Asia this is especially true. Many of the stories which are enacted with the most elaborate dance-like movements originated in India over two thousand years ago, which clearly shows the importance of Indian culture to the South-East Asian region. Some of the ritualistic features of performances reflect ancient animistic beliefs going back even further in time and, even today, the performances can have profound spiritual and symbolical meaning for both the performers and their audiences.

In addition, the culture of the sophisticated courts of South-East Asia affected the development of the theatre. Under royal patronage, traditions were refined, and the aesthetics of their style was dictated by rigid court etiquette. Visually the classical theatre genres are intricately bound to the aesthetic principles prevailing in their respective cultures. Costumes based on old court dress, the stylized postures and gestures of the dancers, and the decorative masks so central to South-East Asian theatre can all still be recognized in the elegant statues and colourful paintings of temples and palaces.

In South-East Asia, as elsewhere in Asia, it is often impossible to draw a clear line between dance and theatre. Most theatre forms are performed by dance movements or with dance-like gestures to the accompaniment of music. The theatrical traditions thus preserve not only ancient forms of literature but also old forms of dance and music.

Apart from the combination of dance and drama, South-East Asian theatre is characterized by the interaction of living theatre and puppet theatre (Plates 1 and 2). Burmese dance developed along with marionette theatre, and some of the most impressive court traditions, such as the *khon* of Thailand and the *wayang wong* of Indonesia emerged from the conventions of ancient shadow theatre.

The living traditions of theatre in South-East Asia have their roots firmly in history. The movements and gestures of the dancer-actors, the stories and their specific language, the musical forms, and the luxurious costumes and masks are based on prototypes that can be hundreds or even thousands of years old. Theatre is, of course, not only of historical interest; the actual performance is always part of the present and the actors are our contemporaries.

1. Arjuna, the ideal hero from the *Mahabharata* epic in *wayang wong* style, performed by Goesti Pangeran Arian Hadikoesoemoe, uncle of the Sultan of Yogyakarta. (VIDOC, Department of the Royal Tropical Institute, Amsterdam, The Netherlands)

Even the strictest and most rigid traditions include comical elements which often refer to the most recent events familiar to the audience. Various levels of time are intermixed. Theatre in South-East Asia has passed through many stages of development, and despite the apparently crystallized form of classical traditions, there is no reason to assume that the tradition will not develop further.

This book is meant to serve as an introduction to the main traditions of dance and theatre in South-East Asia. Chapter 1 discusses theatre and dance as part of the history of South-East Asia—how early contacts with India introduced new elements into earlier indigenous traditions, how this led to the present national styles, and how the traditions have developed in the era of cinema and television.

South-East Asia is the home of hundreds, perhaps thousands, of

2. Arjuna, a *wayang kulit* shadow puppet, Surakarta. (Photograph author)

different forms of theatre and dance, some of which are incorporated in the ritual traditions of small ethnic groups, others at an almost Stone Age cultural level. This book, however, will focus on the classical traditions that are still being performed and can be quite easily seen. The main focus will be on Burma, Thailand, and Indonesia (Chapters 2–5), but there will also be references to Cambodia, Laos, and Malaysia (Chapter 6), where the classical traditions have partly disappeared or are now difficult for outsiders to see.

Along with the Indian influence, Chinese culture has been prominent from time to time in South-East Asia, and there is a significant Chinese population with its own tradition of the performing arts. Chinese theatre in South-East Asia is discussed in Chapter 7, while Chapter 8 reviews the Chinese-influenced theatre of Vietnam.

1   The Layers of Tradition

Roots

SOUTH-EAST ASIA covers the territories of the eastern Asiatic mainland forming what is known as the Indo-Chinese peninsula and the immense archipelago comprising the present Republic of Indonesia, the Philippines, Singapore, and Brunei. The mainland states are Burma, Thailand, Laos, Cambodia, Vietnam, and Malaysia. With the exception of a few islands, this area has for centuries been the meeting point of Chinese and Indian influences. Chinese culture is most strongly present in Vietnam, while elsewhere Indian religions, philosophy, and art have played a decisive role in the development of local cultures.

The culture and theatre of South-East Asia must be seen in the context of a long history marked by international contacts. This, however, easily places undue stress on the role of outside influences. Archaeological discoveries have provided increasing evidence of the long history of local cultures and the presence of early civilizations. South-East Asia clearly had its own, established, cultural traditions long before Indian philosophy and religions found their way into the region, with the ensuing development of Indianized kingdoms from AD 100 onwards.

Traits indigenous to South-East Asia include the cultivation of rice, which led to the so-called rice culture with its own fertility rites, animistic beliefs, and local myths. The early development of metallurgy was also of importance to cultural development in the region, as can be seen, for example, in the development of South-East Asian orchestra forms (Plate 3).

Theatre and dance do not easily reveal their indigenous elements, as the merging of local traditions with Indian influences into the classical theatrical forms took over a thousand years. With its innumerable islands, jungles, and isolated ethnic groups, South-East Asia has been called the anthropologist's paradise. This is no doubt true of theatrical anthropology as well, and many of the rituals and dance forms of small ethnic groups represent features in the development of theatre that have not been affected by outside contacts.

Animistic beliefs were the main forms of religious life in the region before the introduction of Hinduism and Buddhism from India. Animistic cults often involve trance rituals, where the priests and sometimes even the audience fall into a trance and are thus

1

3. Balinese *gamelan* orchestra. (Photograph author)

able to contact the spirit world. While shamanism and other trance rites are common features of most Asian cultures, it is clear that in South-East Asia the trance rites are genuine examples of early indigenous traditions. Buddhism and Hinduism did not break the local animistic traditions; instead, they often assimilated them. Elements of trance rituals could thus be incorporated even into the present classical forms of dance and theatre. In Burma, for example, the dance of the spirit priests often starts a dance or puppet-theatre performance, and in Bali trance rites have been choreographed in this century as part of a new commercial repertoire.

Like the early ritual elements, the musical accompaniment of South-East Asian theatre also represents indigenous traditions. Everywhere in Asia theatre is performed to music, and various theatrical genres have produced their refined musical traditions. It is only in South-East Asia, however, that almost all of the main theatrical forms are accompanied by melodic percussion instruments. Strings and wind instuments may also be included, but the orchestra consists mostly of wooden or stone xylophones, and above all of metal gongs, gong sets, and metallophones. Bronze percussion instruments have a long history in this region. Through trading contacts South-East Asia belonged to the so-called Dongson culture, which was brought to the region from South China

2

and North Vietnam in the first millennium BC. Throughout the whole area, from South China to Bali, high-quality bronze kettle drums of various types and sizes have been found. These were used for ritual purposes.

Even during the heyday of Indian cultural influence, the local musical tradition did not die. The reliefs, in both the ninth-century Buddhist stupa in Borobudur, Central Java, and in the thirteenth-century temples of Angkor in Cambodia depict metal percussion instruments typical of the region today. Development over the centuries led to the present forms of orchestras and their repertoire—the *saing* of Burma, the *pipad* of Thailand, Cambodia, and Laos, and the *gamelan* of Indonesia with their numerous variants.

The role of accompanying music in the overall aesthetics of the theatrical genres is of the greatest importance. One can hardly imagine Western opera or ballet isolated from their musical context. Similarly, the classical forms of South-East Asian theatre have their distinct auditive structures. As elsewhere in regions influenced by India, the dancer-actors in South-East Asia do not always use their voices, but are rather physical representations of the mythical figures expressing themselves with gestures and dance movements. Often the narrator, singers, and chorus in front of the orchestra present the plot and the dialogue. Thus the auditive structure of South-East Asian theatre developed into its specific and unmistakable forms.

While the orchestra creates an elaborate fabric of sound, the dialogues, songs, and comments of the chorus weave ornaments and independent melodic lines adding different emotional levels to the polyphonic whole. On the stage the dancer-actors move slowly, merging—apparently according to their own logic—into the complex structure of the music, songs, and narration. Though the description is highly generalized, it is obvious that because of the musical tradition typical of South-East Asia, the ensuing overall structure of South-East Asian theatre clearly differs from the other major theatrical traditions of the world.

Early indigenous features can also be traced in dance and other movement techniques utilized in performances. In most theatrical traditions in Asia the movement technique makes use of ancient forms of martial arts, and South-East Asia is no exception. The dance movements of the most sophisticated forms of court theatre can still repeat the exercises of warriors from a thousand years ago or the animal movements enacted by hunters of ancient times. Local tradition may also account for the large number of group dances. Solo forms and dance-drama dominate in India, while South-East Asian tradition also includes many slow, processional group dances. Archaic forms of theatre surviving in remote villages can represent relatively unchanged, indigenous styles. On the other hand, complex court traditions may have passed through many stages of development, and do not easily reveal their pre-Indian roots.

Indian Influence

The terms 'Indianization' or 'Hinduization' have been generally applied by historians to the impact of Indian culture upon South-East Asia. As a natural junction of sea routes between Southern and Eastern Asia, this region has had maritime contacts with many parts of Asia since prehistoric times. As ties with India became established, the local ruling classes became involved with Indian civilization. Over the centuries, various cultural traits were adopted, including the Sanskrit language and literature, jurisprudence, and with them a new conception of royalty. The Indianized kingdoms of South-East Asia began to emerge around AD 100, and over the following thousand years a number of kingdoms—which were Hindu, Buddhist, or syncretist, with features of both of them—flourished.

Funan in present-day Cambodia was the first great Indianized power in South-East Asian history (c.AD 100–500). Its traditions were later adopted by the Khmers, who at the height of their power in the thirteenth century dominated large areas of Laos, as well as Thailand and Burma, both of which had had earlier Indianized kingdoms. In the eleventh century the Burmese formed their own Pagan dynasty in Central Burma, and in the thirteenth century the Thais established Sukhothai, their first kingdom.

To the south, the Srivijaya maritime empire reigned from the island of Sumatra. From the seventh to the thirteenth century it controlled the Malay Peninsula, and at times, parts of Java, where in the central region of the island the Buddhist Sailendra and Hindu dynasties had flourished in the eighth and tenth centuries. In Java the tradition of Indianized kingdoms continued until the fifteenth century, when Islam began to spread into the region. The Hindu courts that fled the Islamic invaders established their Indian-influenced culture on the island of Bali. The Indianized culture of South-East Asia acquired increasingly new forms as the dynasties grew, conquered each other, and adopted various accomplishments.

In these Indianized states, it is believed that either the great mass of people were untouched by Indian culture for a long time or they, in absorbing it, changed it by incorporating indigenous ideas and practices. Indian influences were most clearly evident at the court level. It was often court functionaries and Indian Brahmans invited by the ruler who introduced Indian ideas which led to an Indianized court culture, with its conception of god-king, rituals, and artistic traditions. The exalted conception of the monarchy replaced the earlier local, more modest village chief–ruler ideal. Indian ideas of religion and cosmology, such as the concept of Mount Meru, the cosmic mountain, and the central axis of the universe, as well as the four cardinal directions, dictated the forms of temple and palace architecture and even the structure of the court and government.

There were naturally strong Indian influences in theatre and dance, and the classical forms of present-day theatre have retained many of the features they received hundreds of years ago under the patronage of the Indianized courts. Of decisive importance was the adoption of Indian literature, especially the great Hindu epics, the *Mahabharata* and the *Ramayana*. These became the most popular story material for theatre, and have a central role even today, although the small island of Bali is now the only centre of Hinduism in South-East Asia.

The *Mahabharata* could be regarded as the national epic of India. It is the world's largest epic poem, consisting of some 100,000 double verses. Like other great epics, the *Mahabharata*, written in Sanskrit, is a collective work, and its author is unknown. It has been generally assumed that the poem relates events in a period of tribal warfare in Northern India in approximately the ninth century BC. The epic contains elements of the ancient, holy Veda texts, but its final form evolved over the centuries as it was sung by local 'bards' or 'troubadours', who added new details and emphases. The ethic norms of the Brahman class were added to the story, and the *Mahabharata* gradually became a cornerstone of Hindu thinking. In its richness and diversity of levels, the *Mahabharata* is not only an ageless description of ancient clan disputes and bloody warfare, but also an image of an ultimately Indian way of conceiving the world and man's duty in it.

The main action in the *Mahabharata* revolves around the legendary struggle at Kurukshetra between the Kauravas and the Pandavas over land rights (Plate 4). The Kauravas are the hundred sons of Dhrithrashtra, and the Pandavas, the five sons of Pandu, are their cousins. The Pandavas become the heirs to the Kuru throne, since Dhrithrashtra is blind and therefore legally disqualified from ruling. Pandu, however, dies first, and Dhrithrashtra seizes power, though claiming to act as regent for Pandu's son, Crown Prince Yudhisthira, who forms a marriage alliance with Krishna, leader of the Satvants, and assumes imperial prerogatives. Duryodhana, the son of Dhrithrashtra, who is ambitious and envies Yudhisthira's prosperity, invites him for a game of dice, being well aware of his weakness for gambling. Assisted by his father's trickery, Duryodhana wins, while Yudhisthira loses everything: jewels, throne, kingdom, his younger brothers, and finally even Queen Draupadi, the joint wife of the five Pandavas. Draupadi is publicly stripped as a slave by Duryodhana's brother, a humiliation she will never forgive. The elders intervene and arrange terms: Draupadi is restored but the Pandavas are condemned to twelve years' exile and compelled to remain incognito a further year. After enduring this trying time they enter the service of King Virata of Matsya. Yudhisthira now sends Krishna as an envoy to negotiate the restoration of his kingdom, but Duryodhana is not willing to give up even a single village, and so war becomes inevitable. Before the war, Krishna, now acting as an adviser to the Pandavas, and in reality the

4. A scene from the *Mahabharata* showing Abhimanyu (one of the Pandavas) hit by arrows; a *wayang*-style painting in the *kraton* of Yogyakarta. (Photograph author)

incarnation of the god Vishnu, delivers a speech, the famous *Bhagavadgita*, where he encourages Yudhisthira's brother Arjuna to carry out his holy task. A mighty war of justice begins on the plain of Kurukshetra. Yudhisthira marshals his allies against a huge enemy army while the annihilating battle lasts for eighteen days. The Pandavas, after heavy losses and moral concessions, are able to destroy their enemies and Yudhisthira becomes King. Finally Yudhisthira, after hearing of the tragic death of Krishna, retires to the Himalayas, leaving his kingdom to Arjuna's grandson.

In the above, the plot is described only in broad detail. The *Mahabharata* is an immense work with numerous subplots, and hundreds of characters and episodes, out of which independent literary works have arisen. Similarly, in South-East Asia, and especially in Java, purely local variants and dramatizations of the themes of the epic have evolved. In mainland South-East Asia the second great Hindu epic, the *Ramayana*, proved more popular. It tells of the struggle of Prince Rama with the demon-king Ravana. Like Krishna in the *Mahabharata*, Prince Rama is presented as the *avatara* or incarnation of the god Vishnu. The *Ramayana* may have originally been composed collectively, but the legendary

6

5. Nang Sida or Sita, the heroine of the *Ramayana*; a head of a Thai-style rod puppet. (Photograph author)

author Valmiki is mentioned in connection with it. The epic is less extensive than the *Mahabharata*, consisting of 12,000 double verses. The main features of the plot are given below.

Prince Rama goes to a neighbouring kingdom to compete for the hand of Princess Sita (Plate 5). Being the only one able to bend the magic bow, Rama wins Sita as his bride. Rama is about to be named heir to the throne of Ayodhya, but one of the king's wives, referring to a promise by the king, asks that her own son, Bharata, be made heir instead of Rama. The king can only but obey, and thus Rama, accompanied by his loving wife Sita and his younger half-brother Laksmana, is exiled for fourteen years to the southern forest. Here Rama finds the inhabitants harassed by the raids of demons from Lanka, the island fortress of the demon-king Ravana. In the forest, Surpanakha, an ogress and sister of Ravana, falls in love with Rama and Laksmana, but both reject her, and finally Laksmana cuts off her nose. Furious, Ravana plans to avenge the insult. While a demon in the form of a golden deer lures Rama and Laksmana, Ravana in the disguise of an ascetic kidnaps Sita, and flees with her to Lanka. While looking for Sita, Rama helps the monkey Sugriva gain control of the monkey kingdom. In return Sugriva and his loyal monkey army promise to assist in the fight against Ravana. Hanuman, the white monkey, goes to Lanka, discovers where Sita is imprisoned, and gives her a ring, a token of Rama's love. Hanuman is captured and set on a pyre, but with his magic powers he is able to flee, although not before he manages to set the city of Lanka on fire with his burning tail. Rama, Laksmana, and the monkey army invade Lanka, and in the final battle Rama kills Ravana. Sita's chastity is, however, questioned by Rama, and she consents to an ordeal of fire. Unscathed by the flames, she proves her purity. In triumph, Rama and Sita return to Ayodhya, where, the period of exile having elapsed, Rama's noble half-brother Bharata generously surrenders the throne to him.

Indian conceptions of ethics propagated also by the epics affected the hero ideal of South-East Asian literature and theatre. Rulers were often identified with epic heroes, such as Arjuna, Krishna, and Rama. The ideal hero in South-East Asia developed into a figure that is noble, restrained, and aristocratic. Once removed from their Indian context, the epics developed in different ways in various part of South-East Asia. At first, they were recited in Sanskrit, but by the ninth century they had already been translated into some of the local languages. In many parts of South-East Asia they came to be regarded as part of local mythology and literature. A variant of the Hindu *Ramayana* became a national epic in Hinayana Buddhist Thailand. There, Prince Rama is seen as the reincarnation of Buddha and also as the prototype of the ideal sovereign. In Java, which converted to Islam five hundred years ago, the events of the Hindu *Mahabharata* have been so strongly regarded as local history that in the nineteenth century it was still

7

believed that the numerous bone fossils found on the island were the remains of ogres killed in the Great Battle of the *Mahabharata*.

India was also the source of other theatrically important literary material, such as the Buddhist *Jataka* or Birth stories. These are morally instructive stories that came about at different times in various parts of southern Asia, in which the main character is an animal, human, or superhuman being seeking to do good. Within the Buddhist tradition they were gathered into a collection of 547 stories in the Pali language, and the main characters were described as early incarnations of Buddha. The *Jataka* stories became important story material for theatre in the Buddhist states of mainland South-East Asia.

Alongside literary and religious–philosophical themes, Indian influence also affected the techniques of representation adopted by the theatre genres as can be seen in the ruins of the temples of Indianized kingdoms from Cambodia to Java where many of the statues and reliefs show that the dance techniques of the period reflected Indian influence to a great degree (Plate 6). Indian dance and theatre itself had enjoyed a solid tradition over thousands of years in the heyday of the Indianized kingdoms of South-East Asia.

The myth of the origin of Indian theatre shows the central role of theatre and dance in Indian culture. *Natya*, the art of theatre, was the work of God Brahma, the creator, who was asked to give mankind a fifth Veda, which, unlike the four earlier Vedas, could be understood by everyone, even those who did not know Sanskrit. Thus Brahma created the *Natya Veda*, with the assistance of other gods. *Natya* was taught by Brahma to the mythic sage Bharata, who recorded this teaching in the *Natya Sastra*, the manual of theatre. The origin of the book is shrouded in mythology, but the work itself is living reality. The *Natya Sastra* is probably the world's largest and most comprehensive manual of theatre and dance, and is still the foundation of the classical forms of theatre and dance in India.

The instructions of the *Natya Sastra* became established through centuries of practical theatre work. Its present written form dates back to the third–fifth centuries AD, and it gives instructions on almost all aspects of theatre and dance: the theatre building, the stage, the theory of poetry, use of voice, make-up, costume, acting styles, dance techniques, etc. The *Natya Sastra* also presents the theory of *bhava* and *rasa*, so central to Indian aesthetics. It had a profound effect on most of the traditional art forms of India, but, as will be seen, only an indirect effect on South-East Asian theatre. *Bhava* means an emotional state or mood, portrayed by the dancer-actor. *Rasa*, taste or essence, refers to the emotion that the *bhava* performed by the actor should evoke in the audience. The principal aesthetic emotions are nine in number: erotic, comic, pathetic, furious, heroic, fearful, disgusting, wondrous, and tranquil. According to the *bhava–rasa* theory, one of these moods governs any

8

6. Indian-influenced dance scene in the relief of a Borobudur stupa, Java. (Photograph author)

good work of art and although many moods can be involved, one must predominate. This theory applies to poetry, music, painting, and theatre as well as dance.

The *Natya Sastra* defines the techniques of representation that are still in use, of which the dance-like acting technique is central. It must be pointed out that in India, as in South-East Asia, most of the classical theatre forms are enacted with dance movements and symbolic gestures, and dance and theatre are seldom regarded as separate art forms. The classical Indian dance technique described in the *Natya Sastra* is one of the most detailed and complex in the world. It includes 108 basic dance units, 4 ways of standing, 32 movements of the feet and hips, 9 neck movements, 7 movements for eyebrows, 36 types of gaze, and 67 symbolic hand gestures. Thus, the dancer-actor's whole body, from the soles of his feet to his eyelids and fingertips, are trained into a versatile means of expression through years of work.

The use of *mudra*, the symbolic hand gestures, is especially characteristic of Indian dance and theatrical expression. The *mudra* most probably developed from the magic gestures of the ancient Veda rituals. Today in South-East Asia the magical ritual *mudra* are used only in the sacred rites of the Brahman priests of Bali (Plate 7).

In Indian theatre and dance, various combinations of *mudra* permit the dancer-actor to express himself with distinct and nuanced

9

7. Balinese Brahman priest performing tantric *mudra* originating from India during a prayer ritual. (From Jorden Runt, *Magasin för Geografi och Resor*, Stockholm: Natur och Kultur, 1929)

language of gesture. The need for such a form of expression appears to have been based on the fact that the main drama texts were in Sanskrit, which the common people did not understand, while the language of gesture could be comprehended by all. In South-East Asia, symbolic hand gestures are also an essential feature of dance, but they did not develop into a specific gesture language. For example, Khmer, as well as Javanese, classical dance involves only four gestures of the hands, which have different meanings in various contexts or no specific literary meaning at all (Plate 8).

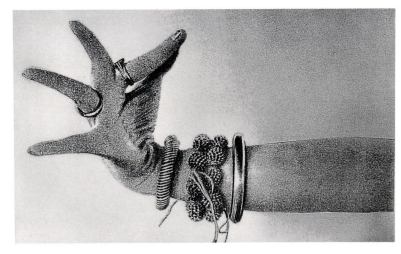

8. An Indian-influenced hand gesture of the Thai–Khmer classical dance. (From Raymond Cogniat, *Danses d'Indochine*, Paris: Editions des Croniques du Jour, 1932)

10

Another important technique, typical of Indian theatre, but utilized to only a small degree in South-East Asia, is that of nuanced facial expression. The facial muscles, eyes, eyebrows, etc., are trained and developed as consistently as the body, hands, and feet. Facial technique is central to the expression of the *rasa* mood, and it can even be developed to the level where the actor can express joy with one half of his face and sorrow with the other.

Purely visual sources do not permit any evaluation of how profoundly Indian theatrical techniques influenced the traditions of the South-East Asian courts. Reliefs and statues, however, clearly depict the open *plié*-like leg positions, energetic footwork, and hand gestures so typical of Indian dance. Indian dance techniques spread to South-East Asia with the court Brahmans. The *Natya Sastra* or other Indian manuals were apparently unknown in the region, nor were they necessary, because the techniques of Indian theatre, as recorded in the *Natya Sastra*, were being developed in practical theatrical work, as it was taught to South-East Asian dancers by Indian teachers. The reliefs of the ninth-century stupa of Borobudur contain several dance motifs, in which many of the dance styles display clear Indian influences. They often portray a bearded male figure—probably a court Brahman—together with dancers to whom he is believed to be teaching the techniques of dance (Colour Plate 1).

The importance of Indian culture to the development of South-East Asian theatre and dance can hardly be overestimated. The plots and religious–philosophical content of many of the genres still display clearly Indian origins. In the techniques of dance and theatre, however, Indian influence varies, but many of the postures, gestures, and movements still echo their Indian prototypes from over a thousand years ago.

Development of National Styles

Direct Indian influence in South-East Asia declined after AD 1000, and gradually new religions replaced Hinduism and Mahayana Buddhism. This brought about profound changes in the South-East Asian culture. The new religions were Hinayana Buddhism (Theravada) and Islam. Hinayana Buddhism began to spread slowly in the sixth century to Burma and later from there to Thailand, Laos, and Cambodia. Further to the south, between the fourteenth and sixteenth centuries, Islam spread from the Malay Peninsula to Sumatra and Java.

The earlier religions, Mahayana Buddhism and Hinduism with their syncretistic combinations, had never really been adopted by the common people, and were mainly practised by the royal families and their courts. Hinayana Buddhism and Islam, on the other hand, rapidly achieved popularity, and they have remained the religions of all levels of society up to the present day. The new religions were adapted to local conditions and earlier beliefs, and so they absorbed elements of indigenous animistic beliefs, as well

11

as Mahayana Buddhism and Hinduism. The concept of the god-king also lived on with only minor changes.

At first, the new patterns of thought had relatively little impact on theatre. The major theatrical traditions had developed under the patronage of the courts, depicting already established classics. The new religions did not basically change the culture of the courts. The ruler was still regarded as divine, his palace was still the centre of the universe, and the artistic traditions of the courts were maintained very much as before. The theatrical traditions were already so established that they could not be broken by new religions, especially as neither of them ever developed styles of theatre that could be described as classical.

Hinayana Buddhism, stressing the role of monastic order and the importance of retreating from the illusions of the world, is more severe than Mahayana Buddhism and has a more ascetic mythology. Furthermore, it reveres Buddha to such a degree that his representation on stage has not always been regarded as proper. Islam, in turn, takes dogmatically negative view of the performing arts. According to the Second Principle of Islam, it is a sin to make an image of man and also to portray him on stage.

The new religions naturally had an effect on the overall atmosphere of local culture, and on the development of theatre as well. For example, Javanese classical dance is believed to have developed its present introverted and restrained character under the influence of Islam. Islam and the new international contacts opened up by it introduced into the Islamized areas new stories, which were soon presented on stage. Through various intermediaries, stories from Arabia, Egypt, Mesopotamia, and Persia were adopted in South-East Asia. In the Hinayana Buddhist countries, on the other hand, the above-mentioned *Jataka* stories became established as one of the most important sources of material for theatre.

The development of the present classical national theatre forms is closely linked to the history of South-East Asia. Although most of the major traditions are those of the courts (Plate 9), they did not develop in a vacuum, isolated from changes in the outside world. On the contrary, contacts between the South-East Asian kingdoms, both warlike and peaceful, have had a decisive effect on the development of styles. Traditions of theatre and dance were valued and envied, and were often seen as treasures of magical sacredness, comparable to royal regalia. Even today, the courts of Java regard their oldest *bedhaya* court dances as sacred heirlooms, and their performances are still the exclusive privilege of the sultan and his court.

It is no wonder that, like the treasures of conquered courts, the dancers, actors, and theatrical traditions were also taken to the conquerors' palaces. In this way, the dance tradition of the Khmer court, conquered by the Thais in the fifteenth century, was adopted by the Thai courts (Plate 10). Similarly, when the Burmese conquered the Thai kingdom of Ayutthaya in the eighteenth century, the originally Khmer tradition was incorporated into the Burmese

9. Balinese court dancer wearing a golden crown and real jewels. (From *Länder och Folk i Ord och Bild*, Helsingfors: Holger Schildts Förlag, 1928)

tradition. Prior to this, when the Thais were at the height of their power, they spread the Khmer tradition into Laos and even into Cambodia, where the style had originated. Each nation, of course, developed the tradition according to its own spirit and national tastes.

Another relatively uniform, and still thriving, performing arts tradition developed in Java and Bali. Although distinctively a tradition of its own, it had early connections with the mainland. Jayavarman II, the founder of the Khmer empire, is known to have had ties with the Central Javanese Sailendra dynasty in the ninth century, from where he is believed to have imported dancers into Cambodia, transplanting the early Indianized dance style of Java to the Khmer tradition. In Java the tradition was first developed in the Hindu–Buddhist courts of Central Java, and later up

13

10. A Khmer-style dancer in a Thai relief. (Photograph author)

to the early sixteenth century in East Java. The Hindu–Buddhist culture of Java came to an end with the spread of Islam from the West, but the old dance and theatre traditions partly survived, being transferred to Bali, where they had a decisive effect on the traditions of this tiny island—today the only centre of Hinduism outside India. In Java the earlier traditions did not die out completely, but were developed further in the spirit of the new dominating religion, Islam, in the *kraton* (palaces) all over the island. Over the following five centuries, this led to the present Javanese classical subtraditions, especially in Central Java.

Apart from the Thai–Khmer style, dominating in most parts of mainland South-East Asia, and the Javanese–Balinese style regarded as the classical style of present-day Indonesia, several minor traditions have also evolved. The Burmese tradition, for example, shares many features with the above, but deriving from slightly different sources, with India as one of its closest neighbours, Burmese theatre and dance have developed their own unmistakable forms. The traditions of Vietnam, the neighbour of Imperial China, on the other hand,

14

strongly reflect the Chinese influences. In practice, the different traditions often coexist and are even intermixed, but in most cases they may be traced. Some regions of South-East Asia, however, never seem to have shared any of these classical traditions, like the Philippines, whose theatre and dance are strongly influenced by the West, first Spain and later the United States.

The Era of Cinema and Television

In South-East Asia the Western colonial period lasted, depending on the country, from the sixteenth century to World War II. It originally had a less drastic effect on the performing arts than, for example, in contemporary British India. Even when stripped of actual political power, the courts continued to develop their art forms, and what is today regarded as the grand classic traditions often achieved their present form to a great extent during the nineteenth and early twentieth centuries. While the Western political hegemony had by that time reached its culmination, Western influence in the arts was mainly indirect; it changed the tastes of audiences, especially the urban audiences, who came into closer contact with the culture of the colonial rulers (Plate 11). This development was supported by some members of the local upper classes and intellectuals who studied in Western-style schools and universities, and sometimes even in Europe, and who were thus able to become acquainted with Western arts and aesthetics, at a time when this was a rare opportunity.

11. *Nang talung* shadow puppets; Western officials among local ladies. (Photograph author)

15

The end of the nineteenth century and the early twentieth century was a period of realism and naturalism in Western theatre and to a great extent in Asian theatre too. The new Western-style theatre houses with proscenium stages introduced totally new, and for the indigenous traditions totally alien, possibilities for Asian theatre, which were usually welcomed as sensational novelties by the urban audiences. The new stage with its sets and painted drops permitted hitherto unseen illusionistic effects emphasized by modern lighting technology (Plate 12). On these urban stages the theatre encountered new audiences and challenges, no longer dictated by the courts and their strict conservatism and etiquette. Many old conventions were suppressed, one of them being the tradition of female impersonators, which had been a common practice all over South-East Asia. Perhaps the demand for stage naturalism to a

12. Traditional Thai *khon* performed with illusionistic backdrops. (Photograph author)

certain degree, and Westernized attitudes, on the other hand, led to the abolition of this practice. This development sometimes went to the opposite extreme, resulting in female actresses impersonating the male characters—as was the established practice in some South Chinese traditions familiar to the Chinese living in South-East Asia. During the period when the present forms of urban popular theatre developed also Western dramas and sometimes even operas found their way to the local stages.

The end of the nineteenth century was a period of emerging patriotism and nationalism, and the new kind of realistic spoken theatre proved to be an appropriate medium for presenting the new ideas (Plate 13). The audiences were often rather small, limited to the educated élite. This practice was continued when most of the present South-East Asian states achieved independence

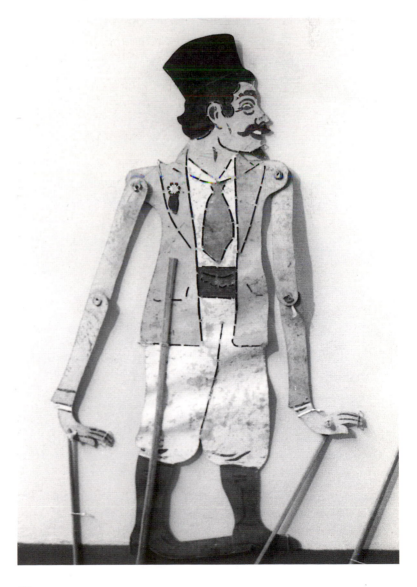

13. Modern politician; Javanese shadow puppet. (Photograph author)

17

around the end of World War II. The new kind of theatre was exploited not only to strengthen national identity, but in some cases to propagate completely new political ideologies. Western-style spoken theatre remains, however, a marginal phenomenon in the culture of South-East Asia, usually finding its keenest audiences among university students.

The old court traditions continued their existence under the patronage of the Royal Households, where these institutions were not abolished, as for example in Burma and Vietnam, which led to the extinction of their old court traditions. In most cases, the present South-East Asian governments adopted the traditions of their former central courts as the national classical styles, which gradually became part of the curriculum of art colleges and universities operating along Western lines, thus making the former palatial traditions accessible to all, regardless of social class. This has led to essential changes. The once strictly ritual genres, whose performances were often restricted to certain definite times and places, are now liberally being performed on modern stages, often those of national theatres, and in many cases they have lost much of their original function. The ever-increasing influence of cinema and the mass media has decreased the popularity of traditional theatre, affecting in some cases its recent developments.

Popular theatre in particular has suffered from the triumph of cinema, which in some cases has completely replaced it. With the rise of the national film industries, many actors began to work in the cinema, and new films have sometimes had a crucial effect on the repertoire of popular theatre, which has had to compete for its audience with the new media. On the other hand, radio and television can in ideal cases serve traditional theatre to reach wider audiences than ever before, although television and recently the video industry have mainly provided the public with predominantly Westernized entertainment.

It is not possible to predict the future of the classical traditions in South-East Asia as so many aims and trends coexist in this field. In many cases they are preserved as a national heritage, suitable to be staged on national occasions and at international festivals. Rapidly increasing mass tourism has led to traditions being adapted into short variety shows suiting the needs of tourists, bureaucrats, and tour organizers, often with disastrous results. On the other hand, much serious work is being done to develop old traditions to suit them better for the tastes of TV-generation audiences. This prevailing 'innovative' trend is, however, balanced by increasing attempts to study and revive the old traditions in their authentic forms.

2 Burma

BURMA is an isolated country, both geographically and politically. It is separated from its neighbours to the west, north, and east by mountains and is bordered by the Indian Ocean in the south. Until the late eighteenth century Burma expanded politically, but the nineteenth and twentieth centuries have been a period of deliberate isolation. As a result, some archaic forms of theatre and dance have been preserved, free from direct outside influences. Burmese theatre and dance did not, however, develop in a vacuum; early contacts with Indian culture played a major role in the development of Burmese classical music and dance, and later contacts with Thailand influenced Burmese drama.

The Burmese are believed to have arrived in their present territory in the ninth century. The former inhabitants of the country were the Pyus, related to the Burmese, and the Khmer-related Mons. The Pagan dynasty (1044–1287) was the heyday of Burmese culture. With its libraries, palaces, and thousands of temples, Pagan was one of the largest Asian cities of its day, and even in the early 1990s it is one of South-East Asia's most impressive ruined cities. The most important ruler of the Pagan dynasty, King Anawratha (1044–77), subdued the Mons and established Hinayana Buddhism as the main religion. Before this, the Burmese had practised Mahayana Buddhism and tantrism along with their own, still surviving, animistic religion, which was developed into its present basic form by Anawratha. The Burmese call their spirits *nat*. Anawratha's religious reforms set the number of *nat* at thirty-seven, and they became loosely linked to the teachings of Hinayana Buddhism. Even at the beginning of the 1990s this early stratum of religion probably has a more institutionalized form in Burma than elsewhere in South-East Asia.

The Pagan culture combined many elements from the Mon and Pyu peoples. The temples and stupas of Pagan display direct cultural loans from conquered peoples; and the performing arts also combined the traditions of the Mons and Pyus (Plate 14). Preserved temple inscriptions suggest that the Pyu and Mon traditions of music and dance were greatly appreciated and were performed along with Burmese traditions. The earliest literary source of Burmese dance and drama deals with the Pyu tradition. According to Chinese annals, the Pyus sent a 32-member group of dancers and musicians in AD 802 as tribute to the Tang emperor of China. The art-loving Tang court greatly appreciated the exotic performances and the

19

14. Ancient-style Mon dance solo, where the performer plays a musical instrument while dancing. (National Museum, Rangoon)

court poets wrote poems of praise in honour of the visit. Wearing their beaded head-dresses, the dancers, accompanied by the orchestra, performed in various line formations and presented dramatic dances enacting the *Jataka* stories. The oldest known Burmese visual source on dance is also related to the Pyu tradition: a group of statuettes from *c*.AD 1000 depicting musicians and a dancer in a lively pose (Plate 15).

The Mongols invaded Burma in 1287, bringing the Pagan culture to a sudden end. The city was abandoned, and the Burmese empire dissolved; the Burmese did not regain control of their territory until some two centuries later. In the intervening period, various Mon- and Thai-related Shan kingdoms arose, but these were finally subdued by the Burmese in the sixteenth century from their capital at Toungo. This marked a new period of Burmese expansion, when the Burmese conquered the Thai capital of Ayutthaya for the first time, taking the Thai king to Burma as their prisoner. Burmese rule extended as far as Luang Prabang in present-day Laos. Like many other South-East Asian kingdoms, the Burmese often moved their seat of power. For a while, the capital was at Pegu, an important

15. Pyu dancer and musicians, statuettes from the National Museum, Rangoon, *c.*AD 1000.

crossroads of sea routes in Southern Burma. In 1635 Ava in Northern or 'Upper' Burma became the new capital. It had been the capital from time to time since the fourteenth century, and it regained this status in 1765. Its name became so closely associated with the whole country that Europeans began to call Upper Burma the 'Land of Ava' and its government the 'Court of Ava', regardless of where the actual capital was. The choice of the new capital anticipated a policy of isolation, as the subsequent capitals were also located inland, far from sea routes.

The eighteenth century was again a period of Burmese expansion. The Mons were banished, and Burmese rule was extended to Dagon in the far south of the country. The town was renamed Rangoon, and later in the early nineteenth century it also became the centre of British rule in Burma. The Burmese expanded their rule as far as Assam and Manipur in India, and the height of their power was reached in 1767 with the sack of Ayutthaya, the Thai capital. The city was completely razed, and works of art, artists, musicians, scholars, and dancers were taken to Burma together with the imprisoned court of Ayutthaya. The Burmese refer to this period as the 'Age of Triumph', and the ensuing epoch is regarded as the golden age of Burmese drama. The *Ramakien*, the Thai version of the Indian *Ramayana* epic, and other drama material were adopted from the Thais. In Burma, the *Ramayana* had previously been known only in the form of the *Jataka* stories. Thai dance and theatre had a great impact on Burmese drama.

21

Burmese culture developed in a rapid succession of capital cities in Northern Burma while Western colonial rule tightened its grip on the surrounding regions. The court culture of Burma (Plate 16) achieved its present forms in Ava (1823–37), Amarapura (1837–59), and finally in Mandalay (1857–85). During this period the Burmese came into open conflict with the British, who ruled over large areas of India. This led to the Anglo-Burmese Wars of 1826, 1852, and 1885. The British first took Rangoon, which became a typical British colonial centre with colossal government buildings of stone, harbours, and parks.

16. Burmese court dress. (National Museum, Rangoon)

In spite of his many attempts at reform, King Mindon (1853–78), one of the most illustrious rulers in Burmese history, was not able to resist the British. In 1886, under the reign of Thibaw, Mindon's son and an incapable ruler, the whole of Burma came under British rule. Eleven years later Burma became a province of British India. The colonial period was a difficult one for both the economy and the culture of Burma. The British exploited Burma's natural resources, and much of the court art with its splendid traditions of theatre and dance disappeared entirely.

Burmese nationalism and patriotism arose in the late nineteenth century, finding initial support among the Buddhist monks (*sangha*), who traditionally had a central role in Burmese society. As elsewhere in South-East Asia, World War II and the Japanese Occupation were politically oppressive times. Burma declared its independence on 4 January 1948, and it became the only country in the world to combine Buddhism with socialism. Political turmoil erupted again in the 1980s when the central government, various power groups, and some of the country's numerous ethnic minorities came into open conflict. Since then, Burma has been closed to foreign visitors from time to time.

Despite the damages of colonial rule to Burmese court theatre, Burma is still the home of many thriving traditions of music, theatre, and dance. India has had a considerable influence on dance and music, although this influence was probably absorbed over many centuries. The Burmese musical tradition, for example, includes archaic instruments of Indian origin that have not been used in India for centuries. Like other major orchestra types in South-East Asia, the Burmese orchestra (*saing*) consists mainly of percussion instruments, gongs, and tuned drums. All traditional forms of Burmese drama are performed by dancing to the accompaniment of an orchestra. The main plot material is from the Buddhist *Jataka* stories and the *Ramakien* of Thailand. Shamanistic ritual performances consecrated to the *nat* are the oldest stratum of the performing arts in Burma.

Ritual Performances: Nat Pwe and Nibhatkin

Most of the traditional forms of Burmese drama still contain ritual elements, but two specific genres are so closely related to religion that they may be called ritual theatre. These are the *nat pwe*, which is related to an animistic cult, and the *nibhatkin*, a Buddhist 'mystery play'. The Burmese have their own versions of indigenous animistic beliefs and practices, which predate the arrival of the Indian religions, Buddhism and Hinduism. As mentioned earlier, spirits are called *nat* in Burma, and in the eleventh century, during the Pagan period, the spirits were canonized. There are altogether thirty-seven *nat*. As in most South-East Asian countries, the new religions of Burma did not do away with older beliefs, thus making it possible for the animistic *nat* cult to survive in strongly Hinayana Buddhist Burma.

Nat may be the spirits of exceptional deceased persons or local variants of the Hindu deities. An example of the latter is Deva Indra Sakka, the king of the *nat*, who can be easily recognized as Indra, the head of the Hindu pantheon. The *nat* are traditionally the protectors of homes, villages, towns, mountains, and forests, although they have also been given Buddhist connotations. They can be regarded as the protectors of the Buddhist dharma, and statues of *nat* are often placed alongside images of the Buddha on temple altars.

The *nat* cult has many features resembling shamanism. A shaman is a kind of priest who is able to alter his states of consciousness through chanting, drumming, and sensory deprivation or mind-altering substances. He can serve as a mediator between ordinary reality and transpersonal realms. Strictly speaking, the term 'shamanism' often means an old form of religion which was practised over a large area ranging from Japan and Korea to Northern Scandinavia. In spreading to the northernmost parts of Europe, monotheistic Christianity destroyed the older forms of religion, and in the same way shamanistic practices have disappeared from the People's Republic of China under communism. In practice, forms of religion that can be classified as shamanistic exist in many places outside the actual shamanistic zone, especially in areas where later dominant religions did not react negatively to older indigenous forms of belief. This was the situation in South-East Asia, where Buddhism, Hinduism, and Islam have in many cases assimilated the strata of animistic religions. In the Burmese *nat* religion, the priestesses, and sometimes the priests as well, fall into a trance, during which they act as oracles or healers to the community that commissioned the ritual. An event of this kind is called *nat pwe* (*pwe*: play). The *nat* shamans are organized, and the *nat* cult is exceptionally well institutionalized despite its ancient animistic character.

The main annual event of the *nat* cult is held at Taungbyon near Mandalay, where dozens of *nat pwe* groups gather for their rituals. These rituals can also be performed at other times, for example, in Buddhist temples, homes, or shops, which are converted into *nat* temples with temporary altars and statuaries. A *nat* ritual is accompanied by a small percussion orchestra, signalling the event with its dynamic music. Fruit, food, cigarettes, beer, and rum are offered to the *nat* statues, after which the *nat pwe* gradually begins.

One or several shamans with their assistants arrive on the scene, dancing in a relaxed manner and partaking of the offerings. The principal shaman performing the actual ritual wears a simple garment, such as a shawl, or a headgear, indicating which *nat* he will be in contact with during the ritual (Plate 17). The shaman dances ecstatically, repeating simple steps and moving his arms and hands in a manner typical of Burmese dance. However, in *nat pwe*, as in other possession rituals, dancing skill is of only secondary importance. The priest sings while dancing and recites scenes from the life of the *nat* being portrayed. At the climax of the ritual, the priest falls into a trance and 'becomes' the *nat* spirit in question.

17. *Nat pwe*; an animistic ritual
    performance, Mandalay.
    (Photograph author)

Still dancing and sometimes writhing half-consciously on the
ground, he tells his prophecies to his assistant, who interprets them
to the audience. *Nat pwe* performances can still be seen frequently,
and a short *nat* ritual is almost always part of a Burmese theatre
or dance performance. The play usually begins with the dance of
the *nat* votaress (Plate 18). In classical productions this dance is
performed by a skilful professional dancer, is more refined than in
authentic rituals and lacks the features of trance.

The Buddhist *nibhatkin* is another form of ritual theatre that has
now become rare. It is a kind of mystery play, in which tableaux
depicting the life of Buddha and his earlier incarnations are taken
from village to village on ox-drawn carts or trucks. This custom
probably developed between the fourteenth and sixteenth centuries
from the *hoza*, the tradition of reciting Buddhist texts. Tableaux
were incorporated into the recitation, and ritual purification, fasting,
and prayers were required of the performers. Comic interludes came
to be added to the *nibhatkin*, and in this way it is believed to have
led to the creation of the *zat pwe*, which enact the *Jataka* stories.
The *nibhatkin* was mainly performed by improvisation, and its
original performing tradition is not known. In the late eighteenth

25

18. The opening dance of a *nat*
votaress, Rangoon. (Photograph
author)

century this theatrical form gave way to the development of
Burmese dance-drama.

A still widely popular ritualistic performance takes place when
young boys and even grown-up men join the monastic order. On
the chosen day, these novices—dressed up as Prince Siddhartha—
will be carried in a procession to the temple area, where their
heads will be shaven (Colour Plate 2).

Dance: Indian Gestures and Puppet Movements

There is only fragmentary knowledge of the early history of Burmese classical dance, but the present dance style probably evolved over some one thousand years, incorporating elements of Mon and Pyu traditions predating the arrival of the Burmese (Figure 1). As may be expected, Indian influences are clearly present, because of the proximity of India, but it is not known in detail how or when Indian influences were adopted.

An important source on the history of Burmese dance is a group of statuettes of Pyu musicians and a dancer from around the year AD 1000 (see Plate 15). The dancer is in a lively position with an uplifted right foot, a bent body, and the left arm bent upwards. The footwork closely resembles Indian dance, and the angular bending of the raised arm is surprisingly similar to the technique of modern-day Burmese dance. In this connection, there is always the risk of overinterpreting the information of static statues and reliefs, as movement—the essential feature of dance—is absent and must be reconstructed. Nevertheless, it seems highly probable that the roots of Burmese classical dance stem from the ancient Pyu tradition.

Burmese dance was also influenced by the classical dance of Thailand, or to be more specific, Thai–Khmer dance; the Thais conquered Angkor in the fifteenth century, abducting court dancers and other artists. The Thais modified the style to their own tastes, and this, in turn, was partly adopted in Burma, when the Burmese imprisoned the Thai court with its dancers after the sack of the Thai capital, Ayutthaya, in 1767. Thai theatre and dance gave new impetus to the performing arts of Burma. During the late eighteenth and early nineteenth centuries, the so-called golden age of Burmese theatre, new drama forms evolved, including marionette theatre, which had a major effect on the aesthetics of Burmese dance (Plates 19 and 20).

Fig. 1
Four of the basic poses for a Burmese female dancer. (Päivi Lempinen)

27

19. Burmese classical dance combining symbolic gestures originating from India with puppet-like movements derived from the marionette theatre. (Photograph author)

20. Burmese classical dance depicting the frozen, puppet-like smile derived from the marionette theatre. (Photograph author)

1. A pair of dancers in identical poses in the relief of a Borobudur stupa in Central Java; the bearded man in front of them is probably a court Brahman and dance instructor. (Photograph author)

2. Procession at Shwedagon Pagoda; boys enacting the events from the life of Prince Siddhartha before entering the monastic order. (Photograph author)

3. Prince, the standard hero of
   the Burmese marionette
   theatre. (Author's collection;
   photograph Hannu
   Männynoksa)

4. Burmese duo dancing in a tourist show in Rangoon.
   (Photograph author)

5. Burmese *pwe* hero on a poster being painted in a park in
   Rangoon. (Photograph author)

6. Dance offering in a Thai temple. (Photograph author)

7. *Nang yai* shadow puppets representing characters from the *Ramakien*. (Photograph author)

8. Training of dancers specializing in the noble male characters at the College of Dramatic Arts, Bangkok. (Photograph author)

9. Training of dancers specializing in the demon roles at the College of Dramatic Arts, Bangkok. (Photograph author)

10. Totsakan (Ravana) from the *Ramakien*; a *khon* mask. (Author's collection; photograph Hannu Männynoksa)

11. Audience scene in Totsakan (Ravana)'s court; a *khon* performance at the National Theatre, Bangkok. (Photograph author)

12. Phra Ram (Rama), Phra Lak (Laksmana), and the monkey army arrive at the battlefield; a grandiose outdoor *khon* performance by the Thai National Theatre. (Photograph author)

13. Angry monkey in a *khon* performance. (Photograph author)

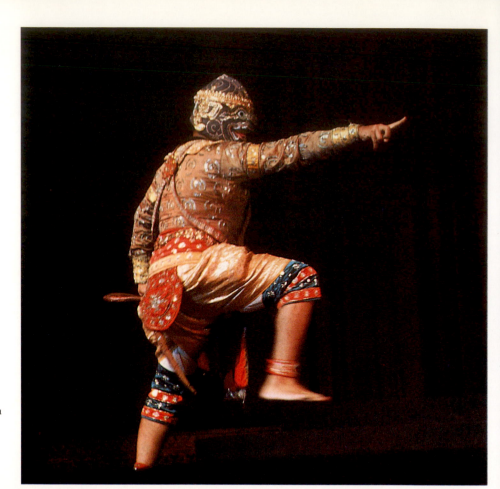

14. The final battle between Phra Ram (Rama) and Totsakan (Ravana) in a *khon* performance at the National Theatre, Bangkok. (Photograph author)

15. *Lakhon nora* or *Manora* dancer from Southern Thailand. (Photograph author)

16. *Lakhon nora* or *Manora* dancer in an acrobatic pose depicting a half-bird, half-human *kinnari*. (Photograph author)

17. A scene from *Inao*; a *lakhon nai* performance at the National Theatre, Bangkok. (Photograph author)

18. A battle between a Burmese hero and a Chinese general in *Saming Phra Ram Asa*; a *lakhon phantang* performance at the National Theatre, Bangkok. (Photograph author)

19. *Nang talung* screen and puppets in the Songkhla Museum. (Photograph author)

20. *Nang talung* clowns. (Collection of Mr A. S. Härö; photograph Hannu Männynoksa)

21.   Thai rod-operated *hun krabok* puppets in the National Museum, Bangkok. (Photograph author)

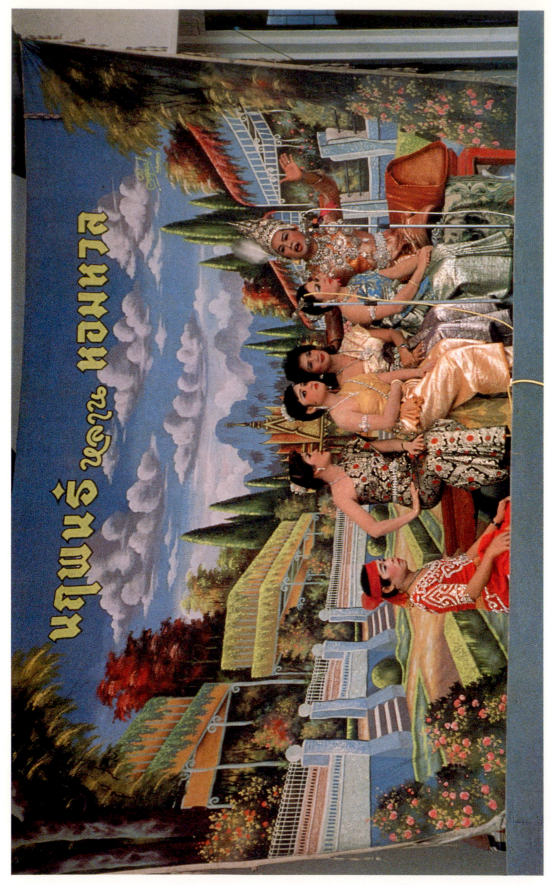

22. *Likay performance in Bangkok.* (Photograph author)

It is generally believed that marionette theatre was developed for enacting the Buddhist *Jataka* stories with their moral teachings. Live dancer-actors were regarded as too impure to portray the principal character, who represents the former incarnations of the Buddha. The art of the puppeteers soon achieved a virtuoso level, and during the century-long heyday of this art form the movements of the marionettes came to dictate the aesthetic standards of live dancers. This explains the jerky, angular movements of the dancers, who often perform sitting or crouching on the floor (Plate 21). The marionette tradition also influenced the way a dancer falls down—like a marionette whose strings have been cut. The performer, however, always falls to the ground in a very graceful position with the legs bent back and the arms bent angularly (Plates 22 and 23). The facial expression is a frozen, puppet-like smile, which also appears to derive from the marionettes. Over the years, various puppet-style dances evolved, emphasizing the precise imitation of marionette movements and gestures.

In the first basic position of Burmese dance, the knees are bent into an almost crouching position, and the body is bent forward with the arms supporting the small of the back. From this 'spring-like' tensed position, the dancer rises from time to time, preserving, however, the z-shaped bent form of the body. Footwork closely resembles the flat footsteps typical of Indian dance, but in Burma the feet touch the ground lightly, sometimes kicking the long train of the costume backwards. The hands repeat gestures of Indian origin, which—unlike the Indian *mudra*—no longer have any precise symbolic meanings. Sharp neck movements accentuate the head movements that follow the rhythm, and the eyes are trained

21. Two dancers in a crouching position. (Photograph author)

22. Dancing prince, stock hero of the Burmese marionette theatre. (Photograph author)

23. Dancer falling gracefully to the ground in the best tradition of the Burmese marionette theatre. (Photograph author)

to the course of the movement. Many dances, or parts of them, are performed in a crouching position, sometimes nearly lying on the ground. There are similar dances in other parts of South-East Asia, and they may have been dictated by the requirements of court etiquette where underlings must kneel before the ruler. Many South-East Asian dances express respect for rulers or are dance-like prayers to Buddha, spirits, or deities.

The present costumes of Burmese dance originated in the courts of the Upper Burmese capitals, where the whole dance style evolved into its present form. The most impressive costumes are direct copies of gilt court wear with flame-like, hanging front parts, sharp epaulettes, and tall, tapering crowns. The standard women's costume includes a narrow ankle-length skirt with a white train. The narrow garment prevents open bends of the legs, which can be seen in Pagan period reliefs of dancers. At present, only the men, wearing the traditional costume of wide short-legged trousers and a rigid, folded loincloth, still dance with open legs. Unlike in India and other parts of South-East Asia, Burmese dancers often wear soft slippers.

In addition to classical dance, the many ethnic minorities of Burma have their own dance traditions. The repertoire of classical dance proper includes various annual festival dances, greeting dances, and dance-prayers. As elsewhere in South-East Asia, the movement patterns and general aesthetics of classical dance are used in all forms of drama. Burmese classical dance is taught at the State School of Music and Drama in Rangoon and Mandalay.

Marionette Theatre: Yokhte Pwe

Burma's highly valued tradition of marionette theatre (*yokhte pwe*) came about in the so-called golden age of Burmese theatre in the late eighteenth and early nineteenth centuries. Its original purpose was to propagate and popularize the instructive *Jataka* stories, and during King Bodawpaya's reign (1782–1819) the Minister of Theatre succeeded in assembling several companies of puppeteers. The origin of the idea is not known, but it is possible that the Thai court, at the time prisoners of the Burmese, also had puppets which inspired the latter to create their own form of puppet theatre. Another possibility is that the Burmese were already familiar with the puppet and marionette traditions of India and China. It has been suggested that the reason for the popularity of marionette plays was the ban forbidding living actors from portraying the sacred personages of the *Jataka* stories.

Several companies of puppeteers were supported by the court and the puppet-masters were highly respected—often more than ordinary actors. The plays were originally created for the court but the touring theatre groups of the rural areas developed their own versions of the classical plays, leading to an amalgamation of court and popular forms. The marionettes, manipulated from above with strings, were about 50 centimetres high. The head, hands, and feet could all move, and in the most complex marionettes, even the fingers could be bent, the eyes closed, and the mouth opened. The most technically developed type of marionette was usually the dancing *nat* priestess or votaress. It is known that in the mid-nineteenth century such a marionette could require up to 60 strings to manipulate its complicated movements. Marionettes of jugglers performed with balls threaded into strings and dancing-girl marionettes could move their breasts and buttocks. Performances lasted all night, and a single play could extend over a whole week. Before the actual performance, offerings were made to Buddha and the *nat*.

The plays follow a definite pattern, the first part presenting the birth of the universe, where the old universe goes up in flames and the following one is deluged. This is followed by a third inhabited by the *nat*. A marionette of a *nat* votaress then performs a skilful dance dedicated to the *nat*. Various animals and beasts appear in their prescribed order, followed by demons enacting their feats. A marionette of an alchemist or sorcerer, one of the stock characters of Burmese theatre, performs conjuring tricks with a wand in his hand. A prince (Colour Plate 3) and a princess, the standard hero and heroine of Burmese theatre, then appear to perform their delicate dance. This is followed by marionettes of the king and his ministers, whose discussion serves as an introduction to the actual play, the second part of the performance. The plots of these plays are derived from the *Jataka* stories and from the *Ramayana*.

Traditional marionette plays were performed to the accompaniment of an orchestra on a wide stage containing a fixed set of a palace

31

hall, with a throne and ritual parasols on the left and a forest scene on the right (Plate 24). The wings of the easily constructed bamboo stage were covered by a pair of curtains painted with scenes of the *Jataka* stories. The puppeteers worked behind the curtain, manipulating the puppets from above the actual stage. A minimum of two puppeteers was needed to manipulate the marionettes, the more experienced one being in charge of the central characters, such as the *nat* votaress and the prince and princess (Plate 25).

The colonial period destroyed much of the traditional theatre, and consequently marionette plays are rare in Burma today. With luck, one may still see marionette plays performed at temple festivals and tourist shows also include marionettes—usually the dance of the prince and princess. After Burmese independence, there have been attempts to modernize marionette theatre along the post-war East European lines, and the puppetry has been used as a medium for new political ideas. Although no longer a thriving art form in Burma, the marionette theatre has had a definite influence on the Burmese dance. The movements and stylized, puppet-like smile of the dancer closely resemble the marionettes and particularly popular are dances where the dancer imitates a marionette dancing alongside it.

24. Burmese puppet stage. (From *Länder och Folk i Ord och Bild*, Helsingfors: Holger Schildts Förlag, 1928)

25. Master and pupil operating the
marionette prince and princess,
Pagan. (Photograph author)

Dance-drama: The National Dramatists

The golden age of Burmese drama in the late eighteenth and early
nineteenth centuries produced not only the marionette theatre but
other forms of drama as well. Court actors from the conquered Thai
capital of Ayutthaya and their refined art inspired the Burmese to
new innovations. The poet Myawadi Mingyi U Sa (1766–1853)
dramatized the Thai *Ramakien* for the Burmese stage. This led to the
Burmese '*Ramayana* play', a danced pantomime broadly following
the conventions of the *khon* mask theatre of Thailand (Plate 26). The
Thai tradition is adhered to in the plots, in some of the dance movements, and in the characters with their costumes and decorative
papier mâché masks, which, however, seem slightly provincial compared with the authentic *khon* masks, whereas the music and dance

33

26. Thai-influenced performance of the *Ramayana*. (National Museum, Rangoon)

techniques are mainly Burmese. The *Ramayana* became established in Burmese tradition, as can be seen in the reliefs of old wooden temples and in Burmese poetry. The spectacular *Ramayana* play, however, has become rare in present-day Burma. In addition to the *Ramayana*, the Thais provided another significant series of stories, the originally Javanese Prince Panji cycle, which is known as *Inao* in Thailand and Burma.

The Burmese drama which evolved around the late eighteenth and early nineteenth centuries had been preceded by the *nat pwe* spirit plays, the comic interludes of the Buddhist *nibhatkin* tableaux, and the *zat pwe Jataka* plays which had developed from the latter. The first secular play, *Maniket Pyazat*, was written by the court poet Padetharaza (1684–1752), but it was only under King Bodawpaya (1782–1819) that Burmese drama began to develop at a faster pace. The king had a special Ministry of Theatre in charge of the performing arts, and the court plays became a kind of state ritual. Burma's main dramatists were U Kyin U (1819–53) and U Pon Nya (1807–66). Many of their works took their themes from the *Jataka* stories, whose moral teachings and fairy-tale character now gave way to a slightly more realistic world and a more psychological portrayal of character. A major reform was the shortening of the dramas from events lasting several nights to performances of only a single evening.

27. A rare historical photograph showing a scene from a Burmese dance-drama of the romantic style. (From Dr Georg Buschan, *Die Sitten der Völker*, Stuttgart, Berlin, Leipzig: Union Deutsche Verlagsgesellschaft, SA; photograph R. Grant Brown)

Three plays by U Kyin U—*Maho*, *Dewagomban*, and *Papahein*, all representing a kind of Burmese classical–romantic style (Plate 27)—have been preserved. U Kyin U's dramas can be performed with minimum stage effects and their language is especially valued for its poetic and emotional qualities.

U Pon Nya developed drama in a more realistic direction. Although the Buddhist law of karma still controls the events, and Buddhist moral precepts still dictate the basic conflict of the plot, U Pon Nya depicts a world that appears to be real, and his characters are psychologically credible. There are still the prince and princess, the stock characters of Burmese theatre, but in U Pon Nya's dramas they are accompanied by a range of 'ordinary', sometimes comic, lesser characters, such as peasants and pedlars. Despite the conventions of the *Jataka* stories, his dramas mirror his times in a colourful and highly detailed manner.

U Pon Nya's major plays are *Paduma*, *Wizaya*, *Kothala*, *The Water Seller*, and *Wethandaya*, the last-mentioned being based on the *Vessantra Jataka*, describing Buddha's penultimate incarnation. *Paduma,* one of U Pon Nya's popularly performed plays, deals with a recurrent theme in the playwright's works: the conflict between good and evil. In this play, the king is warned by his ministers that his seven sons are planning a *coup*, and driven by suspicion, he exiles his sons and their wives to the jungle. The journey through the jungle is a hard one, and the refugees are soon plagued by hunger. The younger princes suggest to their eldest brother, Paduma, that they eat their spouses. Paduma realizes that hunger has driven his brothers out of their minds and when night falls, he flees with his wife. They run through the jungle, finally arriving at a river. There, Paduma's princess-spouse complains of her small feet—she is not

35

used to a life like this. Suddenly, they see a legless and armless man tied to a trunk floating in the river. Pitying the man, Paduma rushes into the water and pulls him on to dry land. The man tells the prince that he is a criminal, who was punished by having his arms and legs cut off and being left to the crocodiles. Paduma sets off to find food for his wife, himself, and the cripple. The princess is greatly interested in the cripple, and immediately makes love to him. She then plans how to get rid of her legal spouse and decides to throw Paduma off a mountain ledge. When the prince returns, his wife carries out her cruel plan, but Paduma manages to catch hold of the bough of a fig tree growing over the river. A friendly crocodile looking for figs takes Paduma on his back and carries him back to his kingdom. The people receive Paduma with great rejoicing, for the old king is now dead, and they want a new ruler. Believing that her husband has died, the princess—in the guise of a peasant woman—wanders back home, carrying her crippled lover in a basket on her back. The people stare in amazement at this beautiful peasant woman, who is brought before the king. The maiden does not immediately recognize her husband, but Paduma recognizes his deceitful wife at first sight. In a rage, Paduma orders the princess and the cripple to be executed immediately. But as it happens to be a feast day, no executions can be carried out, and Paduma, lost in thought, suddenly realizes that it is wrong to kill. He asks in desperation if the execution has already been carried out, but to his joy, he learns that it will happen the following day. Paduma cancels the execution, and banishes the couple for ever from his kingdom.

In *The Water Seller*, U Pon Nya again focuses on the interplay of good and evil within man. A prince is returning home after completing his studies in India. Resting for a moment by the gate of his home town, he is approached by a poor water seller, who tells him how he comes every day to the town to sell water to eke out a living. The man goes on his way, and a girl—another water seller—arrives on the scene, who is even poorer than the first water seller. As the maiden leaves, the prince enters the town, where he is crowned as king. Around noon, the two water sellers meet, fall in love, and decide to get married. The maiden wishes to have a proper wedding, and they decide to pool their meagre savings. The man goes off to find a half silver penny which he has hidden in a crevice in a wall. Defying the hot midday sun, he goes to his cache. The king looks out of his palace window and notices the water seller rushing by in the heat. He calls the man to him and asks where he is going. After hearing of the marriage plans, the king offers the man a half silver penny, but the man still wants to find his own coin. The king then offers the man a hundred, a thousand, and finally a million coins. Still the man wants to recover his own tiny savings, for he regards earned money as more valuable than anything else. The king takes a liking to the water seller, offering him the rank of crown prince and half of the kingdom, and the offer is accepted. The water seller bride, and princess-to-be, is summoned to the

36

palace. In the evening the king wishes to rest in his forest garden and invites the crown prince and princess to accompany him. The king falls asleep, and the crown prince hits upon the idea of killing him in order to gain the whole kingdom. But he is torn by conflicts of his own greed and his gratitude towards his benefactor. The crown prince's better nature prevails, and when the king awakes he confesses his devious aims. Instead of punishing him, the king is pleased by his honesty and offers him the throne. Upon hearing this, the crown prince is even more ashamed and begs the king to allow him to retire into the woods as a hermit, for he has learned that power and luxury corrupt the good in man. The princess arrives on the scene, and after hearing of these events, decides to follow her husband. They go off into the woods to begin a new life as ascetics.

These plays have a distinct basic formula. As in the marionette plays, the first major scene, presenting the conflict, usually takes place in the throne hall of the palace where the king is shown in conference with his ministers. The prince and princess, the hero and heroine, must often wander in the jungle and meet various dangers. The villain of the play, an unethical person, must finally answer for his or her deeds, but the virtuous ruler is lenient, and in almost all the plays the villain retires into the woods as an ascetic, leaving worldly temptations behind him. The plays are usually performed with dance-like gestures using classical dance technique to provide the delicate movement patterns. An orchestra dominated by

28. An outdoor performance of a Burmese dance-drama. (From Dr Georg Buschan, *Die Sitten der Völker*, Stuttgart, Berlin, Leipzig: Union Deutsche Verlagsgesellschaft, SA; photograph D. A. Ahuja)

percussion instruments accompanies the play with the stock melodies of Burmese theatre. As in other parts of South-East Asia, Burmese plays are rarely orchestrated throughout. The musical structure is based on well-known traditional melodies, which the audience immediately identifies with certain dramatic situations, for example, triumphal marches, battles, and lovers' reunions. The actors recite or speak their lines and also sing in the emotionally laden climaxes. The drama texts permit improvisation, especially in the comic scenes.

U Pon Nya was in close contact with the court; he was a personal friend of the king and he wrote his plays especially for the court, where the original manuscripts were kept. Before long, officials in the provinces began to imitate the court, commissioning plays famous in the capital. In this way, the court plays became popular among the common people. Touring theatre troupes created their own versions of the plays, which could be staged in the yards of private houses or in village squares (Plate 28). The troupes performed to the accompaniment of small orchestras. There were no props; a branch could symbolize a forest and a clothes chest could be used for a throne, and the costumes imitated court dress as far as possible. Although full-length performances of U Kyun U's and U Pon Nya's plays are rare today, they are regarded as the national classics of Burmese drama.

The Twentieth Century

In the early nineteenth century the British first gained control of Southern Burma, converting Rangoon into a Western-style centre of colonial rule. In 1866 they finally extended their dominion to Upper Burma. Partly because of the uncompromising attitude of Thibaw, the last king of Burma, court culture was almost completely destroyed towards the end of the nineteenth century. The fate of court culture was sealed when the enormous wooden palace of Mandalay with its court theatre burned down in the final stages of World War II. Burmese court theatre had by this time given rise to a thriving folk theatre, which still reflects lost courtly ideals. Western culture, introduced by the British, had a strong effect on Burma. In the early years of King Thibaw's reign, Western theatre groups had performed for the king himself, and Burma was possibly one of the first countries in South-East Asia to have a Western-type theatre with props and a curtain. A general trend of secularization now permitted live actors to perform even in plays based on the Buddhist *Jataka* stories.

In the 1910s and 1920s Burmese theatre was marked by a cult of star actors, the main figures being Po Sein and Sein Kadon. Po Sein's semi-fictitious biography is one of the few books on Burmese theatre that have been published in a Western language. The star cult developed extravagant forms of promotion, and the actors invented new means to publicize their personalities. Po Sein performed with a 'bodyguard' of two British ex-soldiers, and Sein Kadon sometimes

29. Classical dance performed in a *pwe* 'variety show', Mandalay. (Photograph Leif Lönnqvist)

danced in a costume with blinking electric lights. Despite attempts at sensationalism, their artistic merits were undeniable, and Po Sein bequeathed to posterity not only his repertoire but also a dance style named after him.

When Burma became independent in 1948, the new government began to revive theatre and dance. The theatre was also used to propagate the new political ideology, and East European puppet-theatre specialists were invited to Burma to reshape marionette theatre. Burma has a National Theatre in Rangoon, or at least a group of artists operating under that name, which has toured Europe and the United States. In practice though, it is difficult to see performances, as they are staged randomly, although the State School of Music and Drama in Rangoon and Mandalay strive to maintain the traditions of the performing arts.

Burmese theatre and dance survive mainly in the few tourist shows still being staged (Colour Plate 4), and as part of the entertainment at temple festivals. *Pwe* performances lasting all night are staged in various parts of the country in connection with religious festivals (Colour Plate 5). Large temporary halls and stages of bamboo are erected for the purpose. At dusk, the local pop idols come on to the disco-lit stage to sing their versions of Western and local hits, and tableaux present the climaxes of the newest films. After midnight the classical dancers begin their performance which lasts until morning (Plate 29). In the early 1980s television was still rare in Burma, and movies are seldom presented in the outlying regions. In this context, *pwe* performances serve a number of purposes. The world of cinema, pop culture, folk entertainment, and the remnants of old court culture all coexist in *pwe* performances. The most common ritual performances are the *nat pwe,* which are continuously staged throughout the country.

3 Thailand

THAILAND is a melting-pot of South-East Asian culture. The influence of Chinese and Indian civilization has been felt in the area of present-day Thailand over the millenniums, and the Malay Peninsula provided access to the cultural sphere of Malaya and Indonesia. The Thai tribes are believed to have moved gradually into their present areas from South China. Before they established their rule, the present territory of Thailand was ruled by several small Indianized kingdoms, and some of the areas were part of the Khmer empire. The original religion of the Thais was a form of animism, and the worship of spirits (*phi*) is still very much part of Thai everyday life. From the Mons the Thais adopted Sinhalese Hinayana Buddhism, and through a long process, elements of Hinduism from the Khmers. Thailand is a predominantly Hinayana Buddhist country, but as in many other South-East Asian countries, a syncretist combination of various religions has also evolved there.

The first Thai kingdom emerged in the thirteenth century amidst three thriving dynasties, then at the zenith of their power. In the west was the Burmese Pagan dynasty; in the east the Khmers ruled their empire from Angkor; and in the south the Srivijaya maritime empire based in Sumatra ruled over the Malay Peninsula. The first Thai kingdom was Sukhothai (*c.*1220–1350) in the central parts of present-day Thailand. The Sukhothai dynasty was a period of emerging national identity. Its most famous ruler was Ram Khamhaeng or Rama the Bold, who ruled from the late thirteenth to the early fourteenth century. Under Ram Khamhaeng, Sukhothai ruled over large areas ranging from Laos to eastern Burma, according to preserved inscriptions, his reign was a period of peace and prosperity. Ram Khamhaeng is also said to have developed the Thai alphabet.

Sukhothai was not the only Thai kingdom; in the north was the kingdom of Lanna, whose capital was first Chiang Rai and later Chiang Mai. A Thai kingdom to the south proved fatal for Sukhothai. In the fourteenth century the kingdom of U Thong conquered Sukhothai, from which it had originally seceded. The capital of U Thong, Ayutthaya, grew into one of the most cosmopolitan cities of its day, home to Thais, Chinese, Japanese, and European traders, and Jesuit priests. The name of the city reflects the importance of Hindu culture for Ayutthaya, and is derived from the *Ramayana* epic, where Prince Rama ruled over a kingdom called Ayodhya. This clearly shows that the Sukhothai concept of the monarchy, which still had elements of tribal leadership, had now given way to the god-king ideal, typical of the Indianized kingdoms of South-East Asia. Despite the official Hinayana Buddhism of modern-day Thailand, the ruler is still identified with Rama, and court rituals partly follow Hindu models adopted from the Khmers.

The Ayutthaya period was one of expansion for the Thais. They extended their rule into the Malay Peninsula, and in 1431 conquered Angkor, the Khmer capital. The Thais looted gold and treasure from Angkor, as well as capturing monks, artists, and dancers. Thus, the Thais—via the Khmers—adopted even more thoroughly than before the achievements of South-East Asian Indianized court culture, including the spectacular dance tradition of the Khmers, which was now developed according to Thai tastes. This period also marked Western colonial expansion. Ayutthaya maintained relations with the colonial powers through trade agreements, and managed to keep its independence. Sovereignty was, however, threatened during the reign of Phra Narai (1656–88), when a Konstantin Phaulkon, a Greek adventurer who had become the king's counsellor, plotted to give power to the Jesuits. The reign of Phra Narai, however, is regarded as a period when Thai literature flourished, and the late seventeenth and early eighteenth centuries are described as the golden age of Ayutthaya culture.

Thailand's arch-enemies, the Burmese, harassed Ayutthaya throughout the eighteenth century, and in 1767 they razed the city's gold-roofed temples and palaces, leaving the ruins still visible in the early 1990s. The Burmese now took with them the art treasures, monks, dancers, and court of Ayutthaya to provide a fresh impetus to their own culture. The Thais had done the same at Angkor over three centuries earlier. Ayutthaya was laid waste, but Thai power and culture soon recovered when the Burmese withdrew, and a new Thai capital was established.

The Ayutthaya period was, however, the heyday of Thai culture and the performing arts, and set the standard for later developments. Although most of Thailand's literature was reduced to ashes in the monasteries and palaces of Ayutthaya, and the artists and dancers of the court were taken to Burma, the spirit of Ayutthaya survived. The palaces and temples of Bangkok, the present capital, were modelled after the buildings of Ayutthaya, and Thai classical culture as a whole adopted its ideals from the former capital. Theatre and dance were no exceptions. There is little definite information on the dance and theatre traditions of the Ayutthaya period, but at any rate Khmer-influenced classical dance and shadow theatre flourished. The oldest written source on theatre—concerning the *nang yai* shadow theatre—is from the Ayutthaya period, and it depicts the *Ramayana*, the Hindu epic which gave its name to both the city and the whole epoch.

A few Thai officers managed to flee from the sack of Ayutthaya.

One of them, General Taksin of half-Chinese ancestry, declared himself king, and established a new capital further south at Thonburi, at the mouth of the Chao Phraya River. Taksin was a successful warlord, and in time he subdued the Khmers. Despite his many successes, Taksin suffered a cruel fate: he is said to have lost his mind, and he was executed. He was succeeded by another general, Chakri, who was also half-Chinese and declared himself king in 1782 under the title of Rama I. The choice of name identified the ruler with the virtuous Prince Rama of the *Ramayana*, the incarnation of Vishnu and sole ruler of Ayodhya. The *Ramayana* became the national epic of Thailand, and its most famous Thai version, the *Ramakien*, is attributed to Rama I.

Rama I founded the still-reigning Chakri dynasty. For strategic reasons, he established a new capital, Bangkok, on the opposite bank of the Chao Phraya River from Thonburi. This was the beginning of the so-called Bangkok period, or Rattanakosin era, in Thai history. Through skilful diplomacy, concessions, and modernization, the rulers of the Chakri dynasty were able to preserve Thai independence at a time when all other neighbouring countries fell under Western colonial rule. One of the most important reformist rulers was Mongkut or Rama IV (1851–86), 'The Architect and Champion of Thai Independence', who reformed government administration according to Western models. No less significant was his son, Chulalongkorn or Rama V (1868–1910), who was the first Thai ruler to visit Europe. He has been called 'The Great Reformer' for having abolished slavery, outlawing opium, reforming administration, and creating an infrastructure for it. Thai rule extended beyond the present borders of the country, and Thai culture made its impact on Laos and Cambodia.

While the Thai rulers propagated their so-called Chakri reforms for Westernizing administration, customs, and culture, they were also patrons of traditional culture, and often artists themselves. The history of nineteenth-century Thai theatre parallels the rule of the various kings, and innovations are traditionally attributed to the reigning king. As mentioned above, Rama I wrote the *Ramakien*. Rama II, also a poet, was an active patron of literature. He is known to have had a famous dance troupe, for which he composed music, wrote verse, and even directed its performances. His reign is regarded as the second golden age of Thai theatre after the Ayutthaya period. Rama III, on the other hand, was a strictly religious ruler, who banned the court theatre. The performing traditions were revived by Rama IV, and the performing arts again received legal approval. The reign of Rama V was a period of marked Westernization, when the first Western-style theatre building was built, and realism made its way into Thai theatre. Western theatre and even opera became popular among the upper classes, and a Thai version of Puccini's *Madame Butterfly* was staged. Rama VI revived traditional styles, but he also introduced Western-influenced spoken drama, which was used as a means of propagating nationalism and patriotism. The new types of plays, however, appealed to a limited audience, mainly the intellectual élite. Rama VI also translated Western plays into Thai.

The ruler and the court have been the traditional patrons of dance in Thailand, and the best dance troupes and musicians were employed by the court. The forms of court theatre are closely related to the Hindu-influenced concept of the god-king, while the Hinayana Buddhist orders played only a minor role in the development of theatre and dance. The close ties between the court and the performing arts were severed by the bloodless *coup* of 1932, when the king was relieved of his former absolute power, and Thailand became a constitutional monarchy. In 1934 the arts of dance and music were administrationally transferred from the Bureau of the Royal Household to the government's Fine Arts Department. At present, the classical traditions of dance and theatre are maintained by the College of Dramatic Arts and the National Theatre (Silpakorn Theatre), both in the centre of Bangkok near the old Royal Palace.

Despite formal independence, Thailand could not avoid the turmoil of World War II. A co-operation agreement with the United States was signed in 1950, when King Bhumibol came to the throne as Rama IX. The war in Vietnam strengthened ties with the United States, and Thailand provided 'rest and recreation' for American soldiers. Despite the strong presence of American entertainment in modern-day Thailand, traditional culture still thrives under a Westernized façade, as can be seen in the practice of dance offerings in performances (Colour Plate 6).

In their variety, the dance and theatrical traditions of Thailand reflect the ethnic structure and history of the country. Many of Thailand's ethnic minorities have their own traditions of the performing arts. In North Thailand Laotian influences can be seen, while the dance style of the south has links with the Malay Peninsula. The College of Dramatic Arts in Bangkok and its six provincial colleges have worked to create a 'uniform' style suited to stage performances. The court style of Central Thailand, inherited from Ayutthaya, is still regarded as the classical performing style of Thailand. As in most South-East Asian countries, classical dance and theatre in Thailand is accompanied by an orchestra dominated by percussion instruments, called *pipad* in Thailand. Despite the variety of Thai dance and theatre, performances are difficult to see, or they are staged at random. Classical dance has now become part of the entertainment at luxury restaurants, although the National Theatre and the King Bhumibol Cultural Centre in Bangkok still stage full-length performances and programmes composed of classical dance numbers.

Ancient Shadow Theatre: Nang Yai

The roots of Thai theatre and dance go back to the long-lost traditions of the Mons and Khmers who ruled over the country before the arrival of the Thais. The only information on these ancient traditions is provided by sculptures and reliefs preserved in temples (see Plate 10). Elements of Malay Peninsular, Javanese, and Laotian theatre were also adopted. As there are no written sources, the early history of Thai dance and theatre is impossible to reconstruct in any detail. The oldest preserved reference to theatre is in the Palatine Law from the Ayutthaya period in the 1350s. It refers to the *nang yai*, an ancient and by now almost forgotten form of shadow theatre.

The origin of shadow theatre is a standard problem in Asian theatre studies, as this art form has been practised over a wide area from Turkey in the west to China in the east. In South-East Asia, Thailand, Cambodia, Malaysia, and Indonesia have their own shadow-play traditions. It is certain, however, that shadow theatre employing a translucent screen and static or movable figures is over two thousand years old in Asia; documentary references to this genre have been preserved in China and India before the beginning of our era.

The South-East Asian shadow-play traditions are all closely linked to the Indian *Ramayana* and *Mahabharata* epics. In India their narrative has been accompanied since ancient times by leather puppets, and this practice most probably spread to South-East Asia along with the expansion of Indian culture. How and when exactly this occurred is not known.

The *nang yai* of Thailand is an exceptional and clearly very archaic form of shadow theatre (Plate 30). In most Asian genres of shadow theatre the puppets are rather small, cut human figures with one or two movable limbs. The *nang yai* puppets, on the other hand, are large, 1- to 2-metre-high oval or round non-articulated leather silhouettes, in which the characters are engraved as if in a frame (Colour Plate 7). A large screen, 7–10 metres wide and some 3–4 metres high, is erected on poles approximately 2.5 metres above ground. In front of the screen, with their backs to the audience, are the musicians of the traditional Thai *pipad* orchestra, consisting of oboes, xylophones, gong sets, and other percussion instruments. Sitting among the orchestra are two narrators, who sing the text enacted by the figures on the screen.

The puppeteers move with their figures both in front of the screen and behind it (Plate 31). In Asian puppet theatre the puppeteer usually has a distinctly vocal role, often reciting and singing the lines. In *nang yai* the manipulator acts merely as a dancer, supporting the large leather figure with two poles in his hands. The dialogues and long palace scenes appear to be static, but in the action scenes, the manipulator dances to musical tones of the accompaniment reflecting various moods and basic situations.

30. *Nang yai* performance depicted in the early nineteenth-century murals at Wat Phra Keo, Bangkok. (Photograph author) ▶

31. Dancing puppeteers operating large *nang yai* figures. (Performance sponsored by the Siam Society; photograph Marja-Leena Heikkilä-Horn) ▶

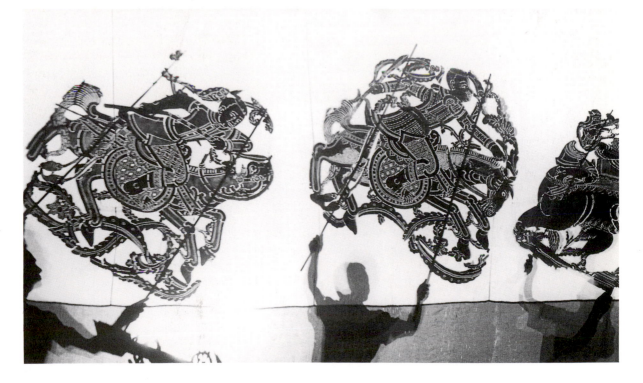

His movements and positions, seen by the audience from under the screen, must correspond to the character of the leather figure. Heroes express restrained masculine energy, demons have strong, open movements, and princesses move with grace and charm. The *nang yai* is thus a relatively complex art form, combining figurative art, the stock melodies of Thai theatrical music, the art of singing and recitation, as well as dance movements.

The most popular, and at present the only, subject-matter of *nang yai* drama is the *Ramakien*, the Thai version of the *Ramayana*. The *Ramayana* found its way into Thailand most probably in the thirteenth century via the Khmer culture, and several Thai versions of it have been written. The oldest ones were destroyed in the sack of Ayutthaya in 1767. The most popular and respected version of the *Ramakien* dates from the end of the eighteenth century, the very beginning of the Bangkok period, and is attributed to Rama I. Rama II also developed the *Ramakien*. The basic structure of the plot is Indian, but the spirit is quintessentially Thai. According to certain theories, the *Ramakien* is not based on the actual *Ramayana* but on a slightly different text with the same theme. The *Ramakien* contains episodes alien to the original *Ramayana*; the tragic turns of the plot have been softened, sensual features have been added, and the role of the faithful monkey Hanuman is stressed. The local colour, customs, and setting of the tale have been given a Thai flavour, and many of the characters have been given Thai names. In the *Ramakien*, Prince Rama, the heir to Ayodhya and the hero of the *Ramayana*, has become Phra Ram. His faithful spouse, Sita, is known as Nang Sida. Laksmana, Rama's half-brother, is Phra Lak; the demon-king Ravana, who kidnaps Sita, is renamed Totsakan, etc. The texts of the stage versions of the *Ramakien* are called *kham phak* (reading texts). The oldest preserved *kham phak* texts, in strict verse, date back to the Ayutthaya period between the seventeenth and eighteenth centuries.

The *Ramakien* is an excellent example of how the Indian epics became genuine local tradition in South-East Asia, and in Thailand it came to be regarded as true national literature. There appear to have been several reasons for the popularity and rapid spread of the *Ramakien*; its ethic code can easily be adapted to Buddhism; and in Thailand it is interpreted as a *Jataka* story describing the earlier incarnations of the Buddha. At the same time it can be linked to the god-king cult adopted from the Khmers. Ever since the Sukhothai period, the Thai rulers have been identified with Prince Rama. Thus, not only is the *Ramakien* an epic of moral teachings but it also has political significance.

Nang yai was originally court theatre, and it had a specific religious meaning; making the puppets and holding the actual performance involved many ritual features. *Nang yai* plays were performed in the evening by the light of coconut-shell fires. The evening performance was sometimes preceded by a prologue in the afternoon—the *nang ram* (*nang rabam*), which was performed in daylight. In the latter, the puppets were painted in bright colours, while the *nang yai* puppets for the evening performances were less colourful. Common to both types of puppets are their decorative style and the portrayal of characters. The leading characters are often depicted as individual figures sitting, walking, fighting, etc. The larger figures may include Rama in his chariot, couples, such as combatants or lovers, or even complete scenes.

At present, *nang yai* drama appears to be in danger of extinction. Since the 1980s it has been performed by only one group of aged players outside Bangkok. The College of Dramatic Arts in Bangkok is trying to maintain the tradition as part of classical dance-drama, where it is sometimes performed as a play within a play. Although *nang yai* can no longer be described as a living form of theatre, it has remarkable connections with the classical forms of Thai theatre and visual aesthetics in general. Preserved in the *nang yai* puppets are the iconographic ideals of the late Ayutthaya period and the early stages of the Bangkok period. The slender, elastic bodies of the heroes and heroines, the costumes, jewellery and ornamental crowns, and the strong demons and lively monkeys are all masterfully chased on water-buffalo hide and can be seen in innumerable temple reliefs and lacquer paintings. The gestures and postures of the figures are repeated in Thai classical dance and in the spectacular *khon* mask drama, which also illustrates the *Ramakien* and is believed to have developed alongside *nang yai*.

Classical Dance: The Thai–Khmer Heritage

According to conservative estimates, there are over a hundred different traditions of dance in Thailand. Many of these are archaic dance rituals or folk dances, belonging to the heritage of small ethnic minorities. The main styles are closely linked to definite theatre traditions, for, as in other parts of Asia, all the traditional forms of theatre in Thailand are performed with dance or dance-like movements. The dance traditions of Thailand can be roughly classed into four main groups: the central, northern, north-eastern, and southern styles. In all Thai dancing, the emphasis is on the movements of the arms, hands, and fingers. The local traditions differ, however, in style. The southern style is characterized by open *plié* positions and expressive finger movements. The north-eastern style incorporates fewer hand movements. The northern style is slow in a legato-like manner, and the central style is characterized by delicate arm and hand movements repeating the figure 8, and a general coolness of courtly elegance.

The central style is regarded as the classical style of Thai dance, and in its refinement it is definitely one of the major dance traditions not only of South-East Asia but the whole world (Plate 32; Figure 2). Thai classical dance is the result of a long development and the fusion of varied cultural elements. According to present

32. All traditional Thai dramas are performed using classical dance movements; a *khon* performance at the National Theatre, Bangkok. (Photograph author)

views, the Thais inherited the dance tradition of the Khmer court when they conquered Angkor in 1431. Khmer dance, in turn, is believed to have been originally influenced by Java. The Khmer court dancers were taken to Ayutthaya, where the dance style changed over the centuries to suit Thai tastes. As in other traditions of court dance in South-East Asia, Indian classical dance is the distant prototype of the Thai–Khmer style. It is the source of many basic positions, hand gestures, and complete series of movements. There are, however, major differences. Indian dance stresses fast, rhythmic footwork, continuously changing facial expressions, and hand gestures denoting express symbols. Thai dance usually has a slow rhythm; the dancers are almost expressionless with arched arms, and the hands repeat only a few extremely decorative, yet meaningful, gestures. By the time it reached the Khmer court, Indian dance had developed a purely South-East Asian style, and under royal Thai patronage it was even further removed from its Indian origins, creating its own inimitable aesthetic.

The Thai language has three words for dance, or specific elements of dance. *Rabam* means a group dance or choreography, *ram* refers to arm and hand movements, and *ten* means footwork. Together, they form the vocabulary of Thai classical dance, although they are emphasized in different ways in the various types of dance. The repertoire of classical dance consists of solo numbers and group dances. Thai dance is usually an inseparable part of the

48

Fig. 2
Three of the basic poses for the noble
male and female characters in Thai
classical dance. (Päivi Lempinen)

classical theatre traditions such as *khon*, *lakhon nai*, and *lakhon nok*.

A student beginning to study classical dance is given a role type corresponding to his or her physique. Thai dance has four main role types with a number of subdivisions. Heroes (*phra*) must be well-proportioned and stately in bearing. This category is divided into major heroes (Phra Ram) and minor heroes (Phra Lak). Heroines (*nang*) are also divided into major (Sida) and minor (Montho) types. The training of dancers to play these characters is based on the *Ram Phleng* (Dancing to Music), the longer of the two basic vocabularies or series of Thai dance. Demons are a specific type, who must have tall and muscular bodies. The simians, central to the *Ramakien* story, must be short and acrobatic. Their basic training involves the shorter series of dances called *Mae Tha* (Mother Postures). Heroes and heroines can be played by either male or female dancers, depending on the style of the performance. Traditions differ in this respect; for example, the *khon* was originally played solely by males, and *lakhon nai* by females. Monkey and demon roles, on the other hand, are played only by males.

The vocabulary of Thai dance is based on the above dance series and their basic movements. The movements have their own lyrical names: for example, the swan walks gracefully, the lion plays with its tail, and the lady sways from side to side. In the early stages of their studies the dancers practise only in seated or crouching positions in order to learn the jerky micro-movements of the torso, the hand gestures, and the precise overall rhythm. They are gradually permitted to dance in a standing position and study the series of dances as a whole. The movements are repeated while reciting their names out loud, which aids in co-ordinating them with the vocal parts. The series are demanding, and it takes about an hour to dance the whole *Ram Phleng* series.

The dance of the heroes and heroines represents Thai classical dance in its most complex form. It makes full use of meaningful hand gestures corresponding to the singing and recitation (Colour Plate 8). The steps are light, although the bare soles of the feet completely touch the floor, while the toes are often turned upwards. As in India and in most other genres of South-East Asian dance, barefootedness is a ritual feature. Footwear was taboo in the palace in the presence of the king, as well as in other sacred places, including the stage. The demi *plié* of the legs permits the characteristic flexibility of movement, the shifting of weight from one side to another, and the small, jerky accents of the dance. The technique of the monkey and demon roles is characterized by extremely open leg position, which is achieved by painful exercises where the teacher helps the pupil to maintain the correct leg position (Plate 33). Classical dance, however, emphasizes delicate movements of the arms and hands. These are practised from the very beginning of the dancers' training by bending the fingers backwards (Plate 34) and by pressing the arms between the knees until they form the desired softly curving shape. In the female roles the movements are usually tuned to a smaller scale; the *plié* is not as marked, nor are the arm movements as open or conspicuous as in the heroes' dances, which are crowned by the impressive raising of the arms in heroic postures. The face remains almost expressionless, and the subdued smile should not reveal the teeth. This is believed to have been dictated by strict court etiquette, which considered spontaneous expressions of emotion as vulgar. The mood is expressed by the sung texts and the accompaniment of stock melodies, as well as by postures and gestures. A hand lifted in front of the mouth signifies joy, and an arched finger is a sign of anger. Conventional gestures and positions can also characterize distinct situations, such as love-making, parting, sleep, and combat. The dances of the heroes and heroines are marked by

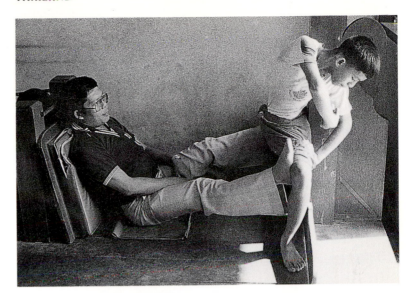

33. A dance teacher helps a young student to maintain the proper open leg position. (Photograph author)

34. The flexibility of fingers and hands; dance training at the College of Dramatic Arts, Bangkok. (Photograph author)

soft gracefulness and strict self-control, both central elements of the aristocratic hero/heroine ideal of Thailand and South-East Asia as a whole.

The heroes and heroines move with legato-like fluency, pausing only briefly for their impressive postures. The demons and simians, on the other hand, combine still positions with playful or vigorous movements. The monkey roles are characterized by acrobatic somersaults and imitations of the natural movements of monkeys, underlined by minor scratching movements and furtive glances (Plate 35). The demons dance with clubs in their hands, and their movements and still positions express aggressiveness and strength (Colour Plate 9; Plate 36). The dancers of the monkey and demon roles learn the shorter series of dances, but they must also be proficient in acrobatics and the martial arts, upon which their movements are partly based.

35. Training of dancers specializing in the monkey roles at the College of Dramatic Arts, Bangkok. (Photograph author)

The standard costume of Thai classical dance is most probably based on the court dress of the Ayutthaya period, although its present form, as well as the standardization of the whole dance style, are often attributed to Rama II (Plate 37). The men's costume consists of calf-length Thai-style trousers wrapped around the waist, a close-fitting long-sleeved upper part, and peaked epaulettes resembling typically Thai roof ornaments. The women's costume is composed of an ankle-length skirt-like fabric wrapped around the waist, and a cloak-like piece of clothing covering the upper body and the shoulders and extending to the ankles. The material of the costumes is bright-coloured silk, embroidered with gold and silver threads and decorated with glittering imitations of precious stones. Glittering rings, chains, and headgear denote the rank of the character. Royal characters wear the tapering and spire-like Thai crown. It adds not only a touch of regality but also an aura of sanctity, as its top resembles the golden stupa-like towers of Thai temples and palaces. The monkey and demon characters wear the same basic costume as the heroes, but they also have full masks corresponding to the style of dress. Dance costumes may

36. Training of dancers specializing in the demon roles at the College of Dramatic Arts, Bangkok. (Photograph author)

37. Demon and beauty in Thai classical dance costumes in a *khon* performance at the National Theatre, Bangkok. (Photograph author)

include as many as twenty-four different parts, and they are sewed on to the performers. The aesthetics of the costumes developed together with the dance style, and their glittering fairy-tale quality is an inseparable part of Thai dance.

Thai dance has spread beyond the present borders of Thailand. It was adopted in Laos and Cambodia during the expansion of Thai power, and it came to Burma when the Burmese abducted Thai dancers in the sack of Ayutthaya in 1767. Despite its many overall Asian elements, classical dance is a quintessentially Thai art form, and its aesthetics developed alongside the visual iconography of the Ayutthaya and Bangkok periods. The reliefs and paintings of the temples and palaces employ dance movements and postures in their depictions of the *Ramakien* characters and other mythical beings. The classical dance style of Central Thailand dominates Thai dance. It has become the most respected form, dictating the standards according to which other dance styles are adapted and developed.

'Masked Pantomime': Khon

Khon is one of the most spectacular forms of South-East Asian dance-drama. It can involve over a hundred actors, a large *pipad* orchestra, narrators, singers, and a chorus. *Khon* is often described as 'masked pantomime'. This is an apt term, for the *khon* actors do not speak their lines; they only enact their characters on stage by using expressive gestures and the whole vocabulary of Thai classical dance. *Khon* plays are always based on the *Ramakien*. *Khon* actors are divided into four main categories and subdivisions, as in Thai classical dance. These are (1) heroes (the major hero, Phra Ram, and the minor hero, Phra Lak); (2) heroines (the major heroine, Nang Sida, and the minor heroine, Montho); (3) demons; and (4) monkeys. Originally all characters wore masks, but since the nineteenth century only the demons and monkeys have worn masks. The *khon* masks cover the whole head and are made of papier mâché, which is painted, lacquered, and decorated with inlaid glass or mother-of-pearl (Colour Plate 10). They are stylistically related to Thai dance costume, and their bright colours and details, such as the shape of the nose, eyes, and mouth and the model of the crown, express the identity and rank of the characters.

Khon theatre has a long history. Rama II (1809–24) is often mentioned as its creator, but it is now believed to be much older. Under Rama II performance techniques were, however, renewed, and more classical dance sequences were added. *Khon* theatre is believed to have originally derived from the Khmer *Ramayana* dramas known as *khol* (monkey). The first written reference to this genre is an account of a *khon* play recorded by a French delegation visiting Ayutthaya in 1691. *Khon* drama is the sum of varied elements. It shares its narrative material, characterization, and movement techniques with the *nang yai* shadow theatre. Many of the conventions of movement are based on ancient martial arts. Before the introduction of firearms, warriors and even members of the court practised martial skills, repeating certain movements series which could also be performed in a dance-like manner. These provided established movement patterns for dance-drama, especially the battle scenes. Another essential feature of the *khon* plays was provided by strict court etiquette, which is maintained in the courts of both Rama and the demon-king Ravana. This practice reflects traditional Thai court etiquette, which *khon* drama propagated to the members of the court and the royal bodyguard, who sometimes performed in the plays.

Khon drama was originally performed outdoors. There was no scenery or stage props, only a few Thai-style podiums with legs serving as seats or thrones. Traditional *khon* plays usually begin with an audience scene, either in Rama's or Ravana's palace (Colour Plate 11). The ruler is surrounded by his court, arrayed according to rank, which is shown by the order of seating or the height of the seat or podium. Behaviour follows strict court etiquette, and no one may stand or walk while the ruler is seated. In the lengthy audience scene the conflict of the story is presented and its preceding events are narrated.

The most spectacular scenes are battles which are often preceded by long negotiations and exchanges of messengers. The *Ramakien* specifically describes ancient battles and conflicts between nobles, which were bound by an etiquette as strict as that of the court. After due preparation, the principal characters and their armies gather at the battlefield (Colour Plates 12 and 13; Plate 38). Rama and Ravana enter from opposite sides of the stage in their traditional gilt Thai chariots with flame ornaments, drawn by men wearing horse masks. Wearing full regalia, they hold their ornamental bows in their hands. Ravana is followed by an army of demons, dancing menacingly and waving clubs. Rama is accompanied by his half-brother Laksmana, and a resourceful monkey army. When the battle reaches its climax, Rama and Ravana step down from their chariots to engage in hand-to-hand combat (Colour Plate 14; Plate 39). Finally, the victor raises himself in a heroic posture on to the thigh of the crouching loser to the acclaim of the audience. The victory scene is an almost picture-like static tableau with exact counterparts in the mural paintings and reliefs of Thai temples.

38. Phra Ram (Rama) and Phra Lak (Laksmana), accompanied by the monkey army, arrive at the battlefield in a *khon* performance at the National Theatre, Bangkok. (Photograph author)

Khon plays are accompanied by a *pipad* orchestra, chorus, singers, and narrators at the side of the stage. The narrators describe the events of the plot and recite with extreme expressiveness the lines of the characters on stage. As in many other Asian theatre traditions, the narrators of *khon* have a central role. They are as vital to the success of the performance as the dancer-actors, who move on stage according to the distinctly spoken lines. Dancing in Thai dance-drama can be divided into two types: gestures illustrating the text, and dance proper to a musical accompaniment. Both types are fully used in *khon* drama.

Khon plays have a duration of several hours, and they describe only a single episode of the *Ramakien*. Over the years, *khon* texts have been adapted into different versions, some of which have become especially popular. One such version is *The Floating Lady*, which is attributed to Rama II. It is an appropriate example of a *khon* plot for two reasons: first, it is quintessentially Thai, that is, it does not belong to the original Indian *Ramayana*, and secondly, its language is highly valued for its poetic qualities.

In this episode, Totsakan (Ravana), blinded by passion, ponders how to get hold of Sida (Sita), the object of his love. The episode begins with an audience scene in the court of Totsakan, where Totsakan's niece Benyakai claims that she can transform herself into Sida's double and thus fool Phra Ram (Rama) and Phra Lak

39. The final battle scene of the *Ramakien* in a *khon* performance at the National Theatre, Bangkok. (Photograph author)

(Laksmana). Benyakai leaves for a moment, and returns before Totsakan as Sida's double. The enchanted Totsakan cannot restrain himself, and starts to make advances to the maiden. Benyakai changes back into her own self, and the embarrassed Totsakan apologizes for his behaviour. Benyakai sets out upon her mission, assuming her magical disguise as Sida. She enters the water and floats up the Godavari River to a place where Phra Ram bathes every morning. Phra Ram is sleeping in his camp, and awakes at dawn. Amidst the sounds of the early morning Phra Ram marches down to the river for his morning bath. As he approaches the river, the apparently dead body of Sida floats upstream. Phra Ram is shocked at the sight of his dead beloved. After much lamenting, he turns to Hanuman, the general of his monkey army, who is not, however, so easily taken in by tricks and appearances. Hanuman wonders how a dead body could float upstream against the current, and he suggests that the body should be immediately cremated. The pyre is prepared and the body is placed upon it. Unable to bear the heat, Benyakai, in the guise of Sida, flies up into the sky, closely pursued by Hanuman, who with his supernatural powers is also able to fly. The episode ends in a fabulous scene, where Hanuman pursues Benyakai through the heavens, catches her, and finally makes love to her.

Khon drama has experienced many changes. It was originally performed solely by males with female impersonators playing the women's roles, but in the present performances of the National Theatre of Thailand, women's roles are usually played by female dancers. The main changes, however, have been in stagecraft and scenery. *Khon* plays were originally performed outdoors without props or sets, but in the nineteenth century, along with the increased popularity of realism and the new Western-style theatre houses, *khon* plays began to be performed on a Western-type proscenium stage with illusionistic, fairy-tale like scenery. The heavily painted sets, however, easily reduce the subtlety of the fine-toned dance sequences. This stylistic conflict is the same as in many Bangkok period wall paintings, where the ornamental silhouette figures of traditional Thai art are placed in ponderous romantic settings or in palaces shown in perspective. Modern lighting techniques are also used, including spots and even stroboscopic lights. The most interesting attempts to reform *khon* drama do not involve its outward forms but its content. The *Ramakien* is a large work of literature, and the *khon* plays usually illustrate only single episodes. Like many other South-East Asian forms of theatre, *khon* is of an epic nature. It usually presents a series of events, and does not focus on individual psychological features. In recent years there have been experiments where the text has been adapted and compiled to portray the life of an individual character such as Hanuman or Piphek, the brother of Totsakan.

Khon was originally a form of court theatre with strong sacred connotations, but after the revolution of 1932 this union was dissolved. Previously, its tradition had been interrupted only under the puritanical reign of Rama III. Despite all these changes, *khon* drama has retained many of its ritual features. In the actors' dressing-room is an altar where the masks of the mythical Teacher or Master Rishi and some of the *Ramakien* characters are revered. There is a similar altar at the side of the stage, where offerings are made before the performance. The actors make a respectful gesture of greeting before donning their masks, and the same gesture is made to the stage, which is regarded as sacred. The National Theatre of Thailand is at present responsible for maintaining the *khon* tradition. It stages from time to time traditional and innovative *khon* plays, and in connection with state festivities the *khon* troupe of the National Theatre arranges grandiose open-air performances. The theatre groups of the universities perform more liberal interpretations of *khon* drama.

Forms of Dance-drama: Lakhon

Lakhon is an overall term referring to many forms of dance-drama in Thailand. It is believed to derive from Java, where the plot of a performance is called *lakon*. The most archaic genre of *lakhon* is *lakhon nora* from the Thai part of the Malay Peninsula; the most classical form is *lakhon nai*, developed in the courts of Ayutthaya and Bangkok and originally performed by royal maidens; and the popular form is *lakhon nok* originally performed by men. In the nineteenth century international influences and theatrical realism led to even other forms of *lakhon*. The various genres differ in plot material and in some performance techniques. While *nang yai* and *khon* illustrate the events of the *Ramakien* and are quite epic in nature, only one of the *lakhon* genres bases its plots on the *Ramakien*. In the others, the plots are derived from the ancient *Jataka* stories and folk-tales (Plate 40). The *lakhon* plays thus have a distinct fairy-tale character.

The southern *lakhon nora*, also known as *lakhon jatri* or *Manora*, is stylistically quite different from the other forms of dance-drama, which developed mainly in Central Thailand. Its dance style stresses angular movements, very open leg positions, and extremely expressive finger movements emphasized with long detachable fingernails decorated with beads (Colour Plate 15; Plate 41). The technique includes a unique way of moving by sliding the feet instead of walking. The music and movement techniques have strong Malay–Indian flavour, and the characteristic, demanding acrobatic poses have preserved ancient Indian dance poses (*karana*) that disappeared in India centuries ago. *Lakhon nora* groups originally consisted of only three male actors, but today women may also become *lakhon nora* stars, and groups may include several members.

The standard plots of *lakhon nora* plays were derived from two sources: the *Ratsen* and the *Manora*, of which the latter has been more popular. It tells of a supernatural *kinnari* (half-bird and half-

40. Ritual performance of the folk-style *lakhon* in the Temple of City Pillar, Bangkok. (Photograph author)

41. Expressive dance gestures of a *lakhon nora* dancer, typical of South Thailand. (Photograph Marja Leena Heikkilä-Horn)

human) princesss named Manora, who, like other *kinnari*, lives on the mountaintops of the Himalayas (Colour Plate 16). One day a hunter sees Manora and her sisters bathing, and is struck by her beauty. He steals her wings and tail, and takes the maiden to a palace, where the crown prince falls in love with her and marries her. The prince, however, has to go off to war, and an evil minister convinces the king that Manora must be burned in order to save the king's life. Manora is placed on the pyre, but at the same moment she regains her wings and flies back to her heavenly kingdom. After many trials, the prince acquires supernatural powers, and is allowed to enter the kingdom of the *kinnari* and rejoin his loved one.

The tale of Manora is also known in Central Thailand, where it developed into a classical dance-drama (Plate 42), as well as in Cambodia, Burma, Malaysia, and Indonesia. *Manora* was originally a Buddhist *Jataka* story, and the prince is actually the Buddha in one of his earlier incarnations. The story is rather complex, and it requires many evenings to be completely presented. In practice, the story is used only as a binding theme, and the whole performance includes prayers (Plate 43), dance numbers, obscene verbal humour,

42. *Manora* dance in Central Thai style. (Photograph author)

61

43. A *lakhon nora* performance usually starts with prayers. (Photograph Marja-Leena Heikkilä-Horn)

folk comedy elements, and sometimes magic rituals intended, for example, to bring bad luck upon some rival theatre group. The *lakhon nora* dancers have traditionally had an aura of magic about them, which may refer back to the roots of the genre as a kind of shamanistic healing ritual.

The standard costume of the *lakhon nora* dancers consists of shin-length trousers, a bodice of bright, woven glass beads, and a heavy, tapering crown (Plate 44). A distinctive feature is a bird's tail or wing-like extension in the back of the costume, which probably derives from the half-bird *kinnari* of the *Manora* story. Only the clown character, Phra Bhun, dances in a relaxed manner

44. *Lakhon nora* dancers, wearing shin-length trousers, bodices of bright woven glass beads, and heavy tapering crowns. (Photograph author)

in a white loincloth, with a grotesque, red half-mask leaving the mouth free for the lines (Plate 45). *Lakhon nora* was originally performed outdoors without props or sets. At present, the touring troupes usually hang a painted backdrop with illusionistic scenery behind their small stage.

Lakhon nora is a strange relic among the various forms of theatre in Thailand. It has its own music tradition; its language is a Southern Thai dialect; its movement techniques appear to have come almost directly from far-off India; and it has an undeniable magical character. Its origin has been the subject of much speculation. According to one theory, it is the link between the ancient theatrical forms of the Malay Peninsula and the *lakhon* of Central Thailand, and possibly the basic form of the other *lakhon* types. It has also been claimed that *lakhon nora* separated from the Central Thai tradition at an early stage, developing in isolation. Whatever its origin, it is a unique theatre tradition in its inimitability and

45. The red half-mask of Phra Bhun, the clown character of southern *lakhon nora*. (Photograph author)

expressiveness. It is being preserved as part of the cultural heritage peculiar to South Thailand, which, except for occasional performances in Bangkok, is the place to see *lakhon nora*.

Lakhon nai is the most classical form of *lakhon* dance-drama (Colour Plate 17). It developed in the courts of Ayutthaya and Bangkok, and its name means 'the inner or intramural theatre'. Its history may be longer, possibly going back to the ancient dance-drama of the Khmers. The first written reference to *lakhon nai* however, comes from the Ayutthaya period. It was performed by the royal maidens of the king's harem, and the performances could be viewed only by the king himself, his guests, and members of the court. It was not possible to use male actors in *lakhon nai*, as it was performed in the women's quarter of the palace. At the beginning of the Bangkok period the Thai kings still kept large harems, to which vassals 'donated', mainly for political reasons, their beautiful daughters, who were taught classical dance in the palace.

In *lakhon nai* the plots are based on three story cycles: the *Ramakien*, the *Unraut* relating to the Hindu god Krishna, and the most popular one, the originally Javanese *Inao* which was adopted in Thailand at an early stage. *Inao* is a Thai version of the extensive cycle of stories relating the adventures of Prince Panji of East Java. It tells of the separation of Prince Panji, or Inao, from his beautiful bride, and the many adventures they experience in trying to find each other. The actresses recite their lines in gentle voices, but the demanding vocal sections are performed by a female chorus to the accompaniment of a traditional, percussion-dominated orchestra playing variations of stock melodies.

Lakhon nai utilizes the glittering standard costumes of Thai dance and the whole vocabulary of classical dance, of which the actresses must have full command. The dance style is approximately the same for both men and women, and there are thus no technical obstacles to women playing men's roles or vice versa. When women perform as male characters, the masculinity of the dance is toned down, and the all-female cast gives the *lakhon nai* its characteristically graceful femininity. The early stage of the Bangkok period was the golden age of *lakhon nai*, but Rama III outlawed it as well as other forms of court theatre in the first half of the nineteenth century. The *khon* mask drama recovered from this brief ban, but it was difficult for *lakhon nai* to survive, and it lost popularity in the late nineteenth century when realism came to the fore. At present, the College of Dramatic Arts in Bangkok and the National Theatre of Thailand maintain both traditions, although *lakhon nai* performances are rarely staged.

Lakhon nok is a popular form of dance-drama, which, unlike *lakhon nai*, is mainly a product of the common people, and it is closely linked to the Buddhist temple fairs, although the palace also had its own *lakhon nok* groups. It was originally restricted to male actors, usually professionals. Since the early nineteenth century women have been permitted to perform in female parts. There are dozens of *lakhon nok* plays, usually dramatized versions of the Buddhist *Jataka* stories or folk-tales. Here, as in all genres of *lakhon*, the performances have a distinct fairy-tale quality. The plays depict the trials of noble princes, and adventures in demon-infested forests with Hindu deities and spirits taking part in the action.

A very popular *lakhon nok* play is a dramatization of *Phra Law*, an ancient story of tragic love, which is known to all Thais. It has been attributed to King Boromo Trailokanat (1448–88) or King Narai (1657–88). It is a tale of a young prince, Phra Law, who is handsome and loved by all. He is married to a princess equally perfect, but a mysterious restlessness erodes the prince's peace of mind. Driven by these feelings, he flees his palace, finally arriving in the kingdom of his father's enemy, where he meets two princesses. They fall passionately in love, and the princesses hide Phra Law in their chambers, where they enjoy complete and perfect happiness. The girls' grandmother finds out that the son of her arch-enemy is hiding in her palace, and orders her servants to kill Phra Law. In the ensuing fight, all three young people are tragically killed. During the cremation ceremonies, the two enemy kings, the fathers of the victims, become reconciled.

Sang Thong, based on widespread Asian legend, is another popular plot in *lakhon nok*. Its earliest Thai version dates from the Ayutthaya period in the seventeenth century, but the commonly used drama version is from the beginning of the nineteenth century, when Rama II and his court poets adapted the tale to court tastes. In Act One of the intricate story, the hero Sang Thong is supernaturally born in a conch shell. He is in fact a god incarnated in a conch shell in the womb of a childless queen. The queen's strange childbirth is the subject of much attention at court, and an evil concubine plots with the court astrologer to eliminate the queen. Reluctantly, the king banishes his consort to a forest, where the saddened queen cherishes her conch shell in the hut of a poor couple. One day, the spirit of the forest decides to help the queen by enticing Sang Thong out of his shell. There is no limit to the queen's surprise when she discovers a beautiful little boy on the steps of the hut, whom she recognizes as her own son. In Act Two, the evil concubine hears of Sang Thong, and drugs the king with aphrodisiacs so that he orders the boy to be killed. The king recovers too late from the spell; to his horror he discovers that his son has already been drowned. In Act Three, Sang Thong, who had been cast in the water, finds his way into a kingdom of monsters, where he is looked after by a childless demon-queen, who in human form loves Sang Thong like her own child. But she cannot give up her monster's habits, and regularly visits the world of humans to catch people for her food. Sang Thong spends 15 years among the demons, until one day, when his foster-mother is hunting for human flesh, he becomes curious and enters the forbidden rooms of the palace, despite her express orders. To his horror, he finds in these rooms bones and remains of human bodies, which reveal his foster-mother's true nature. He goes on to find a golden well where the water turns his finger into gold. He also finds a black man's disguise, and a magic wand and shoes of crystal enabling him to fly. In Act Four, Sang Thong flees the palace, but the demon-queen, yearning for her son, looks everywhere for him. Finally, the heartbroken foster-mother dies of her own sorrow, but not before blessing her son with a secret charm. In Act Five, the ageing king of Samon faces a problem. He must find suitable husbands for his seven daughters, and decides to arrange an audience for all the eligible men in his kingdom. To her father's dismay, the youngest princess, Rochana, does not wish to choose any of the candidates. In Act Six, the perplexed king asks if there is an eligible man left in the kingdom, and he hears of a strange black man living in the forest. Reluctantly, the king has the man—Sang Thong in disguise—brought to court. To her parents' horror, Rochana gives her consent by throwing a white garland on to Sang Thong's crystal wand (Plate 46). The young couple is banished to a forest hut, where Sang Thong reveals himself as a divine prince to his bride, and they become husband and wife. In Act Seven, the king plans a way to get rid of the black man, and arranges a fishing competition for his sons-in-law. The one who cannot bring back a hundred fish to the palace must forfeit his life. The confident husbands of the six daughters set out with their servants. Sang Thong, now in his divine form, uses

46. Rochana gives her consent by throwing a white garland on to Sang Thong's crystal wand; a *lakhon nok* performance of *Sang Thong* in the Ram Khamhaeng University, Bangkok. (Photograph author)

magic to put a spell on the fish, promising to break the spell only if the men cut off the tips of their noses. Horrified, the men agree to this and downheartedly return to the palace with their fish. The princesses faint when they see the shame brought upon their husbands. After a short while, to everyone's dismay, Sang Thong, again disguised as the black man, comes to the palace with a large catch of fish. In Act Eight, the god Indra, high in the heavens, discovers the humiliation of Sang Thong and Rochana. Indra sends a heavenly messenger to challenge the men of the court of Samon to a polo match. If the court players lose the match, the kingdom will be destroyed. The six fear-stricken sons-in-law lose the match, and only when Sang Thong is brought to the game is victory assured. When they see Sang Thong in the form of a handsome prince, the king and queen of Samon regret their former acts. In Act Nine, Indra comes down to earth to Sang Thong's father and urges him to find the banished queen. The king finds his wife in a hut in the forest, and she forgives him for all the wrongs he has done. In the guise of commoners, they wander into the kingdom of Samon, where they serve in the royal court. The queen uses secret messages to reveal her true identity to Sang Thong. Their reunion is a joyous one, bygones are forgiven, and Rochana, Sang Thong, and his parents leave for their own kingdom.

Sang Thong, like other *lakhon* plots, is very complex, and the actual performances usually consist of only one or two acts, as the overall context is known to the audience. *Lakhon nok* has many features in common with *lakhon nai*, although its music has a faster tempo, and dance skills of a classical standard are not necessarily required. There are also differences in the vocal parts, for unlike *lakhon nai*, this tradition permits the dancer-actors to sing themselves. The costumes in *lakhon nok* are based on classical dance attire, although some characters, such as Sang Thong in the black man's disguise, wear masks. At the peak of its popularity at the end of the nineteenth century, *lakhon nok* was being performed in almost a hundred casino-theatres around Bangkok. It was naturally affected by the tastes of the common people, with a stress on comic aspects (Plate 47) and a free interpretation of the theme. The sets make full use of illusionistic effects with painted backdrops and modern lighting. The National Theatre of Thailand and theatre groups in the universities still perform *lakhon nok* from time to time.

47. Comic female impersonators in a performance of *Sang Thong*. (Photograph author)

The age of Western theatre and cinema led *lakhon* to develop in a more realistic direction, creating *lakhon phud* or spoken *lakhon*. There was also an operatic, completely sung, form of *lakhon*. During the reign of Rama V (1868–1910) Thai classical dance was revived, although it received strong foreign influences at the same time. This led to *lakhon phantang*, where foreign influences such as 'ethnic' costume and Chinese martial arts were adapted to basically Thai-style dance-drama. A well-known example of the *lakhon phantang* style is a play called *Saming Phra Ram Asa*. It is part of a larger work called *Rajathiraj*, describing the many conflicts between the Burmese and the Chinese in the fifteenth century. The various nationalities wear their own costumes; for example, a Chinese general, displaying his martial arts in the fighting scenes, is dressed in Chinese opera costume (Colour Plate 18). Thus, one branch of *lakhon* developed as a historical play with its requirements of naturalism and 'local flavour' in much the same way as Western theatre in the nineteenth century.

Puppet Theatre as Folk Art: Nang Talung and Hun Krabok

Along with the ancient *nang yai* shadow theatre described earlier, Thailand is the home of two other forms of puppet theatre, the southern *nang talung* shadow theatre and the rod-puppet theatre called *hun krabok*. In these forms of drama the repertoire is mostly derived from the *Ramakien* (Plate 48), but as forms of popular theatre *nang talung* and *hun krabok* have had to adapt to the tastes of their audiences, and other stories have been included in their repertoire. All forms of puppet theatre, however, have retained ritual elements, such as initial prayers and offerings to the puppets. Both *nang talung* and *hun krabok* require a group of some ten performers, including the leader who usually acts as the main manipulator and narrator, his assistants, and the orchestra. The stage is a small hut of bamboo, matting, or corrugated iron. The puppeteers and the orchestra sit inside the hut separated from the audience by a white screen in *nang talung* or behind a translucent painted backdrop in *hun krabok* (Plate 49), from where the puppets are manipulated.

The *nang talung* shadow puppets vary in size from 15 centimetres to almost 50 centimetres. They are made of translucent calf hide, painted in bright colours (Colour Plate 19). The figures are usually cut in full face form, unlike, for example, the puppets in Indonesian shadow theatre. In most cases, at least one limb—but often several limbs as well—can be manipulated unlike in *nang yai* where the puppet is a static image. Older existing puppets display a typological development from solemnly decorative *nang yai*-related figures to a less restricted comic-strip style. Along with the *Ramakien* the repertoire of *nang talung* includes plots borrowed from *likay* folk opera and from cinema, and the puppets may portray Western

48. *Nang talung* shadow puppets, representing figures from the *Ramakien*. (Photograph author)

49. A scene from a *hun krabok* performance of the *Ramakien*. (Photograph author)

officers, operetta heroes and heroines, or even cowboys. However, the popular principal characters are always the stock clowns, such as Ai Noi, Ai Tong, Ai Muang, and Ai Klang (Colour Plate 20; Plate 50). They present obscene humour, often characteristic of *nang talung* and always loved by the audience. Each has its own characteristics: one is constantly moving its mouth, while another has a phallus-shaped index finger, and a third has negroid features.

The *nang talung* puppets are often simply, or even coarsely, executed. On the other hand, the three-dimensional, rod-operated *hun krabok* puppets reflect the aesthetics of classical dance and the *khon*. They are even made by the same artisans who make the *khon* masks. The material, papier mâché, is common to both and the puppets are skilfully painted and decorated with gilded lacquer and pieces of mirror. The costumes, gestures, and movements of the puppets imitate classical dance. *Hun krabok* has become very rare, although it is sometimes shown on television. It was originally popular even in the court, as shown by the impressive collection of puppets in the National Museum of Thailand in Bangkok (Colour Plate 21; Plate 51). *Nang talung* is still being performed in Southern Thailand in the Pattalung district, although cinema and television have eroded its former popularity.

50. Some of the many comic figures of *nang talung*. (Photograph author)

51. Rod-operated *hun krabok* puppets
in the National Museum, Bangkok.
(Photograph author)

The Twentieth Century

The preceding sections have touched upon a few historical factors that were essential to the development of Thai theatre in the twentieth century. The main one was the breaking of formerly close ties between the royal family and the performing arts. The rulers of the Chakri dynasty were influential in the development of theatre and dance in the nineteenth century, and the reign of Rama II (1809–24) is still regarded as the unsurpassed 'golden age' of Thai theatre. He was followed, however, by the puritanical Rama III, and in the mid-nineteenth century court theatre was banned. This led to a situation where the performance tradition of *lakhon nai* nearly died out. Under the reign of reformist rulers at the end of the century, traditional Thai theatre came into competition with spoken drama and even Western opera. Admiration of Western art introduced realism and naturalism, undermining even more the role of traditional stylized Thai theatre, especially as Western-type stages, illusionistic sets, and lighting effects were adopted. These features were stylistically alien to Thai classical theatre.

As in many other Asian countries, Thai theatre at the turn of the century became a platform for patriotism and nationalistic ideology. Western-influenced realistic theatre was seen as the most

52. *Likay* performance in Bangkok.
(Photograph author)

suitable medium for these aims. At the same time, intellectuals became familiar with Western drama. Under Rama VII (1925–35), traditional Thai theatre found itself in a serious crisis. The main reason was an economic depression, which limited the court's resources for maintaining expensive forms of theatre. Around this time, cinema, the modern rival of traditional theatre, gained popularity, and the first commercial movie theatre was established in Bangkok. A decisive turn of events occurred in 1932, when royal power was limited, and Thailand became a constitutional monarchy. This signified the final break between the court and traditional theatre, which was now under the authority of the government's Fine Arts Department. The old traditions gradually came to be regarded as national art instead of the court art as which they had been created and developed.

Since the end of the nineteenth century new audiences have influenced the development of theatre. The *lakhon nok* performances of the commercial theatres were mainly aimed at the urban bourgeoisie, and plays at Buddhist temple fairs usually drew a rural audience. Theatre had to adapt to the tastes of a new kind of audience, and the ideals and severity of court art gave way to new melodramatic plots and less refined humour. The most popular form of folk theatre was *likay*, a kind of 'folk opera' which had

73

probably developed in the nineteenth century (Colour Plate 22; Plate 52). In *likay*, the music, histrionic techniques, and costumes also include Indian and Malay elements. The plots may sometimes be borrowed from *khon* or *lakhon* repertoire, but they are mostly quasi-historical melodramas with separated lovers, children who are lost and then unexpectedly found, amorous intrigues, and such similar material. The actors rarely have any extensive degree of training, and the classical dance numbers are usually only alluded to. Microphones are used for the lines, and the serious lyric verses are sung. Sets consist of garishly painted backdrops portraying, for example, palace halls, gardens, or forests. The costumes are a blend of different epochs with glittering sequins, synthetic brocades, and the men's plumed head-dresses, all lending an unreal operatic flavour to the whole. At the height of its popularity, *likay* was performed in several competing theatres in Bangkok, but towards the end of the twentieth century it can mainly be seen on temporary stages at temple fairs or amusement centres.

Cinema and television are naturally the main rivals of both classical and popular theatre. The new media have provided employment for many actors who began their careers in the theatre, but the flood of Western films and the thriving video business are serious threats to the Thai motion picture industry, which—at least artistically—is still on a very modest footing. Fortunately, the government's Fine Arts Department and the College of Dramatic Arts, as well as its provincial colleges, maintain the classical dance and theatrical traditions of Thailand and thus provide thousands of young people with the opportunity to study their demanding techniques.

4 Indonesia: Java

THE long history of Java, the central island of the Republic of Indonesia, is marked by international maritime contacts. The island is a natural crossroads of the sea routes between East and South Asia, and it has been the melting-pot of cultural influences for thousands of years. This is clearly evident in the island's rich traditions of theatre and dance. The present classical forms of drama and dance were created by the Islamic courts of Central Java over the past two hundred years. They combined old indigenous traditions with mythical story material and classical dance technique from India. Yogyakarta and Surakarta in Central Java and the capital, Jakarta, in the western part of the island are today the main centres of Javanese dance and theatre.

Several early Indianized kingdoms typical of South-East Asia flourished on the islands of Indonesia. The first of these was the Srivijaya maritime empire on the east coast of Sumatra, which controlled trade in the Malacca Straits from the seventh to the thirteenth centuries. Culturally, Srivijaya carried on the heritage of Funan, an early kingdom in mainland South-East Asia. Srivijayan dominance was also felt on the island of Java, where in the eighth and ninth centuries the Mahayana Buddhist Sailendra dynasty and its contemporary, the Hindu Sanjaya dynasty, ruled. Since both competing dynasties flourished in the central parts of the island, this epoch is generally known as the Central Javanese period.

The history of the Central Javanese period is not known in detail, but the fact that the dynasties created some of the finest temples in all South-East Asia clearly reflects the level of their civilization. Around the turn of the eighth century and in the early ninth century the Sailendra rulers built the magnificent ziggurat-like stupa of Borobudur. With its hundreds of Buddha statues and thousands of reliefs, it is one of most important monuments of the Buddhist world. The Sanjaya dynasty began to build South Indian-influenced Hindu temples in the Central Javanese highlands from the eighth century onwards. The most impressive monument of Hindu architecture in Java is Prambanan from the early ninth century—a vast complex of 156 shrines built around eight major temples, with the temple tower of Shiva as its dominating feature.

While the basic concept of both Borobudur and Prambanan is Indian, both monuments have many features of both indigenous and Indian traditions forming a unique synthesis. The rich sculpted reliefs of the temples are an invaluable source on the history of the period, and especially dance and theatre. At both Borobudur and Prambanan, numerous reliefs with dance themes have been preserved, reflecting strong Indian influences. Most of the reliefs depict the postures of Indian classical dance. Alongside the dancers are bearded figures, who appear to be directing the performance. These have been interpreted as Indian Brahmans invited to the Javanese courts, who, along with other duties, taught Indian dance techniques. The reliefs also reveal many local features of the culture. For example, some dance themes have been interpreted as depicting purely indigenous traditions. In addition, the portrayals of orchestras represent the local traditions of percussion ensembles and their music, known in Java and elsewhere in Indonesia as *gamelan*.

Indianized court culture is not believed to have extended at first beyond the ruling classes. The Hindu deities and the Mahayana Buddhist concept of the Bodhisattva were blended with local animistic beliefs, which marked the beginning of a typically Javanese syncretism combining different religions and beliefs. India was also the source of the central Hindu epics, the *Mahabharata* and the *Ramayana*, which were adopted along with religion, Sanskrit literature, architecture, and dance technique. As in other South-East Asian countries, the epics were translated into the vernacular and became national classics. They were often narrated to larger audiences using shadow puppets to visualize the stories, which had been the custom in India since ancient times. Shadow theatre or *wayang kulit* is still the most popular form of classical theatre in Java.

For reasons that are still unknown the Central Javanese period came to a sudden end in the early tenth century. The Kingdom of Mataram rose to power, East Java became more prominent, and the ensuing historical phase is known as the East Javanese period. The stupa of Borobudur, Prambanan, and other temples were left in the jungles to bear witness to a period that may be described as the classical, Indian-influenced stage of Javanese history. In the East Javanese period, the immediate influence of India declined, and local elements arose. One of the most significant rulers of the Mataram kingdom was Airlangga (1019–42), who extended Javanese rule even to neighbouring Bali, thus initiating the gradual Javanization of this small island and other areas. The Javanese rulers waged war as far as Vietnam, Cambodia, and even China. Sanskrit texts were still actively translated into Javanese. New story cycles, still popular today, were created, for instance, the famous poem *Arjuna Vivaha* written in honour of King Airlangga's wedding. In religious life, the tantric teachings of India gained influence, adding yet another element to the syncretism of Javanese religion.

In 1292–3 Java was briefly invaded by the Mongols, whose aim was to make Java recognize the overlordship of Kublai Khan. After this interlude, the Majapahit dynasty (1293–c.1520) came to power, the last of Java's major Hindu dynasties. The fourteenth century was the heyday of Majapahit rule. Areas of Sumatra and

West Java were conquered, and Bali again came under East Javanese rule. This was an active period of court culture and the arts in East Java. The dance and theatre traditions of this period are not known in any great detail, but shadow theatre and other forms of drama are believed to have been actively performed in the East Javanese courts. Bali, having adopted the East Javanese tradition, is still the home of some of these art forms. The architecture of the East Javanese period clearly differs from the Indian influences of Central Javanese times. The East Javanese temples are ziggurat-like mounds dominated by split gate-towers. The style of the temple reliefs and sculptures also differs from the Indian classical ideals of the Central Javanese period. The East Javanese style is known as the *wayang* style, as the portrayal of human figures is closely related to the stylization of the *wayang kulit* shadow puppets. The figures in the reliefs are usually shown with the face in profile and the shoulders in frontal position just as in the shadow puppets. The costume, crowns, and jewellery also correspond to East Javanese shadow-theatre traditions, which by now had found a new home in Bali. The *wayang* style in its many variations remained the central style of the traditional visual arts in Bali and Java until the twentieth century.

Majapahit power gradually declined in the fifteenth century with the spread of Islam, and Malacca, the first of the South-East Asian sultanates, rose to power in the Malay Peninsula. Islam spread gradually into Java, where Demak, the first Islamic centre, began to break away from Majapahit rule. In 1527, together with its neighbouring towns, it succeeded in crushing the Majapahit dynasty, bringing to an end the Hindu East Javanese period. According to legend, Islam was introduced into Java by nine holy men (*wali*). The most famous of these was Sunan Kali Jogo, who is believed to have spread the teachings of Islam by shadow-theatre performances of the Hindu *Mahabharata*. This legend clearly demonstrates the specific features of Islam in Java. Instead of wiping out earlier beliefs, it assimilated them. This led to a syncretistic religion typical of Java, which combines animism, Buddhism, Hinduism, and Islam and has had a clear effect on the arts, including theatre and dance. As before, the ruler was regarded as divine, and the cult of the god-king and court culture retained many Hindu and Buddhist features of earlier times.

After a period of dynastic warfare, the Mataram dynasty came to power, and Central Java again rose in political influence. One of the most important sultans of this dynasty was Agung (1613--45), whose court in Yogyakarta ruled over the whole of East Java and other regions. Still existing dance forms, such as the slow ceremonial *bedhaya*, and the *serimpi* female dances, as well as many mask and martial dances are known to have been performed in the court of Mataram. In the sixteenth century the island of Java had begun to interest Westerners seeking spices. In 1602 the Dutch established their trading company, the Vereenigde Oost-Indische Compagnie (VOC), which led to a long period of Dutch hegemony on the islands of Indonesia. In 1619 the town of Batavia was founded at the site of the former village of Jayakarta. This miniature Amsterdam became a major port of trade and the centre of Dutch rule. The British were the main competitors in these areas, and they succeeded in acquiring rule over Java from 1811 to 1816. After Dutch rule had been re-established, the actual colonial period began in 1830, when the Dutch gained control of the whole of Java.

The Mataram dynasty expended its energies in the Javanese Wars of Succession. In 1755 the dynasty split into two, and two capitals Yogyakarta (Yogya) and Surakarta (Solo) were founded only a few dozen kilometres from each other near the ancient Central Javanese temples. In both cities the most important part is the *kraton* (also known as *keraton*), the sultan's palace enclosed by walls and forming a city within a city. The symbolic features of the plan of the *kraton* clearly reflect ancient Hindu and Buddhist cosmology. The outermost parts of the *kraton* were reserved for the army and the court officials and their families. The interior consisted of several open administrative buildings serving various ceremonial functions. The sultan resided in the most protected central part, and, in accordance with old Hindu–Buddhist custom, he was regarded as divine.

In the early nineteenth century the royal families of Yogyakarta and Surakarta again divided, leading to a politically precarious situation where the two capitals were simultaneously ruled by two sultans in each. When full political power was taken over by the Dutch, the ruling families of Java concentrated their energies on refining court etiquette and on developing the arts, especially theatre, dance, and music. This led to a unique renaissance of the arts, in which the classical genres of Central Javanese theatre and dance found their present forms.

The rise of nationalism among Javanese intellectuals in the early twentieth century anticipated a period of political turmoil which was later inflamed by World War II. The Japanese ousted the Dutch and occupied Java from 1942 to 1945. On 17 August 1945, after the end of the Japanese Occupation, Indonesia declared its independence. Yogyakarta was for a short time the temporary capital, and the seat of government was later moved to the Dutch-built city of Batavia, now renamed Jakarta. The Republic of Indonesia was established in 1950 with Dr A. Sukarno as its first elected president.

Java is the centre of the Republic of Indonesia consisting of over 6,000 inhabited islands. It is also the centre of the world's largest Muslim state, with a population of approximately 200 million. Indonesia has innumerable forms and genres of theatre and dance, but the main, classical styles are to be found in Java and Bali. For over a thousand years, *wayang kulit* shadow theatre has been the core of Javanese theatre, influencing the development of other genres. Over the centuries, the various sultanates with their *kraton* have developed their own art forms by adapting and combining ancient Hindu–Buddhist traditions in the spirit of Islam. Java is also the home of various classical forms of *gamelan* and dance styles, of which the most important ones are the West Javanese style (Sunda), the East Javanese style, and the Central Javanese style, whose best-known traditions were refined in the *kraton* of Yogyakarta and Surakarta. The Central Javanese dance style can be described as the most classical dance style of Java. During the period of Indonesian independence the dance style of Java and its theatre traditions have spread to other islands, forming a kind of pan-Indonesian style.

The World of Shadows and Puppets: Wayang

Wayang kulit (*wayang*: literally shadow, sometimes puppet; *kulit*: leather or skin) is still the most popular form of shadow theatre in all Asia. It has been extremely important in the development of Javanese theatre, as most of the other forms of classical theatre have derived their story material, stylization, and many performing techniques directly from it. *Wayang kulit* set the aesthetic standard of Javanese theatre, and partly Balinese theatre as well. The stagecraft and equipment are relatively simple; the *primus motor* being a single puppeteer or *dalang*, manipulating the leather puppets on a simple white screen and acting as a narrator to the accompaniment of a *gamelan* orchestra (Plates 53 and 54). It is, however, an art form of immensely rich and intricate symbolism and philosophical content. Shadow drama gave rise to other forms of puppet theatre, for example, *wayang klitik* with flat wooden puppets and *wayang golek* with three-dimensional rod puppets, which are discussed at the end of this chapter. Although these forms of theatre are highly developed, and *wayang golek* still thrives, they are clearly surpassed by *wayang kulit* in popularity and complexity.

As mentioned in the section on ancient Thai shadow theatre, the origin of the art of shadow theatre in South-East Asia has been the subject of much speculation. There are two theories concerning the roots of Javanese shadow theatre. According to one, it came from India together with the *Ramayana* and *Mahabharata* epics during the long process of Java's Indianization. The other view maintains that Javanese shadow theatre has ancient indigenous roots. This is often supported by the fact that part of the shadow-theatre repertoire is based on pre-Hindu story cycles, and that all the technical terms of the genre are Javanese and not derived from Sanskrit or other Indian languages. The earliest record confirming the existence of shadow theatre in Central Java dates from AD 907. In the East Javanese period shadow theatre is believed to have been adopted by the Hindu courts of Bali during the long process of its Indianization. The Balinese puppets still bear strong resemblances to the so-called *wayang*-style reliefs in East Javanese temples, which are believed to have shared a common style with the contemporary East Javanese shadow puppets. Present-day Javanese shadow puppets are, in turn, believed to have evolved into their extremely elongated and almost non-figurative style during the period of Muslim rule, thus reflecting Islam's ban on making a human image.

53. *Wayang kulit* puppets seen through the white screen. (Photograph author)

54. *Dalang* at work; *wayang kulit* ▶
     screen seen from behind.
     (Photograph author)

The story or plot of *wayang kulit* as well as other Javanese drama performances is called *lakon*, roughly meaning the course of events or action. The plots are derived from various sources, for example, the *Mahabharata*, the *Ramayana*, the Prince Panji cycle, and later Muslim stories. The four oldest cycles, dealing with the ancient history of Java, are collectively named *wayang purwa* (*purwa*: primeval, original, ancient). This includes both pre-Hindu exorcistic material and *lakon* based directly on the *Mahabharata* and the *Ramayana* epics, whose heroes are regarded as the mythical ancestors of the Javanese. Sometimes the *lakon* are faithful to the original texts, but in many cases the epic heroes have been removed from their authentic contexts and have been written into new, purely Javanese, fantasies.

There are several hundred *lakon*. They serve merely as guides to the performances, including lists of scenes and personages, and descriptions of the action in the actual play, which in practice includes a great deal of improvisation not written in the *lakon*. *Lakon* follows a more or less standard structure. The play begins with audience scenes in the palaces of opposing monarchs, where the main conflict is presented. In the ensuing sections, the opponents send messengers to each other until they finally meet in person. Whilst preparing for the battle, the hero will experience many doubts and inner conflicts. The climax is a great battle, which is also a drastic turning-point in the action. Finally, the victorious noble hero presents himself in his full glory at the home palace, and the plays usually have a happy end, the obligatory victory of the right. The themes are highly ethical, and the mood is generally serious, although the whole includes comic scenes with stock clown characters, slapstick, and even topical satire. Javanese theatre thus combines highly noble qualities with earthy comedy and even obscene grotesqueness.

Wayang kulit is to a great degree the art of the narrator. The performance of the *dalang* is the focus of the whole, often 10-hour-long performance, which traditionally begins at 9 p.m. and ends at sunrise. The *dalang* is also responsible for the rituals performed in connection with the play, and he must know by heart the main *lakon*, which are in a way revived with the addition of much improvisation. The *dalang* have traditionally had a priest-like role, and the profession passes on from father to son. Today, *dalang* are also trained in special schools, but they are still highly respected members of their communities, the best *dalang* being famous throughout the island.

The *dalang* thus carries on the ancient oral tradition passing on the main body of classical literature, but at the same time he must be able to improvise and add even the most topical items to the whole. He must also be skilled in recitation, singing, the vocal characterizations of the roles, and the elevated and vulgar levels of the language, along with manipulating the puppets in front of the screen. Moreover, the *dalang* displays expert knowledge of the music so essential to the performance. He leads the *gamelan*, an ensemble of up to thirty musical instruments: gongs, metallophones, xylophones, drums, flutes, zithers, and stringed instruments along with a chorus of female singers. One set of metallophones carries the recurrent melody, which is elaborated by other metallophones, xylophones, and gong sets, with the drums conducting the rhythm, while another set of metallophones gives the *dalang* his pitch. The *gamelan* accompaniment is indeed an integral part of the performance. Each principal character has his or her own musical theme or leitmotif, and the *gamelan* drastically accentuates the three decisive turning-points of the performance, changing from the rather low-keyed accompaniment of the beginning to an ever higher pitch and faster tempo towards the end.

The *wayang kulit* puppets, skilfully cut and chased in leather, are in themselves works of art following strict iconographic rules (Colour Plate 23; Plate 55). A single performance may require the use of 100–500 puppets, varying from some 20 to 100 centimetres in height. The body of the puppet is usually depicted *en face*, but the face and feet and the extremely long movable arms and hands are in profile. The different characters, as well as their social status and psychological qualities, are marked by the size, colour, and other details of the puppet. There are, for example, fifteen eye shapes,

55. Sita and Rama, Central Javanese *wayang kulit* puppets. (Photograph author)

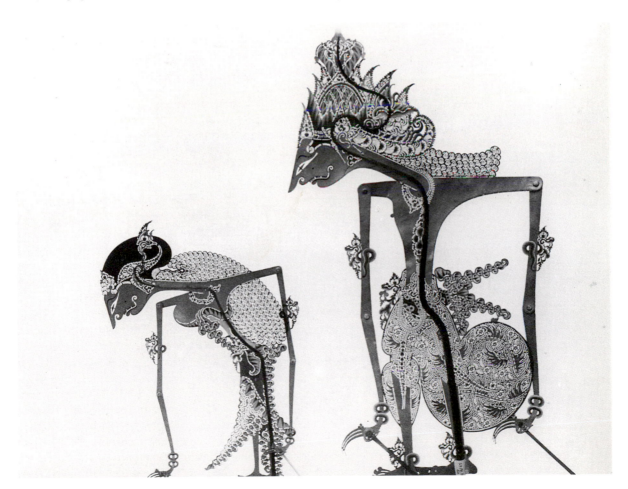

thirteen nose shapes, and eleven mouth shapes, which together with specific costumes, head-dresses, crowns, and jewellery typify the characters. The noble, so-called *alus*, characters are usually small, the strong *gagah* characters are larger, and the demons full of aggressive power are the largest.

Like the genre as a whole, the puppets of *wayang kulit* form an endlessly rich world of their own, a kind of science, which to an ever-increasing degree leads the initiated viewer into the secrets of the '*wayang* world'. The noble hero puppet, for example, follows the Javanese hero ideal of utmost beauty. His body must be slender and well-proportioned, his nose long and pointed, and his eyes must be shaped like soy beans. He must also look downwards, a reference to self-control and humility, the greatest virtues of South-East Asian heroes. The stronger characters may look straight ahead, and the more arrogant ones may even look upwards. The noses of the strong characters point upwards, and they have round, bulging eyes. The requirements of the male hero also apply to the royal princesses, whose refinement is taken to the extreme. Colour symbolism gives added detail to the characterization of the puppets, specifying their mood or temporary emotional state. Gold, the dominating colour, indicates dignity and serenity; black is a sign of anger or maturity; red is for tempestuousness; and white is the colour of youth. To make matters more complicated, the principal characters can be presented with several puppets during a single performance, according to situation, mood, or age. For example, Arjuna of the *Mahabharata*, the Javanese hero *par excellence*, has thirteen different puppet shapes.

Some of the puppets are revered as sacred objects, and they can even belong to the sacred court heirlooms called *pusaka*. One of the most sacred puppets of a *wayang kulit* set is, surprisingly, not a noble hero but Semar, the head of the servant clowns or *panakawan* of the ethically good party. Semar is old, fat, short-legged, and flat-nosed. He is far from noble or handsome, but his eyes are those of a wise and kind person. With his soft breasts and round rear, he is regarded as a hermaphrodite, the 'father and mother' of his servant sons, the long-nosed Petruk, the limping Gareng, and the shy Bagong (Plate 56). The servant clowns assist the most noble heroes, and they are permitted to utter the most daring jokes. The mood of a performance usually becomes intensified when they appear on the screen. Semar is basically seen as a god in the guise of a clown, who helps the hero achieve his goal with kindness and humour. The origin of the *panakawan* has led to much speculation. It is maintained that they are old indigenous deities, which have been adapted to later Indianized mythology. This suggestion is supported by, for example, the stylization of the Semar character which differs drastically from the other puppets. On the other hand, clowns play a central part in almost all forms of theatre in South-East Asia. This is also the case in Indian drama where the *sudraka*, a noble-born but lazy Brahman acts as the king's adviser. However, clowns rarely have roles as central as those of Semar and his sons

56. Semar (*right*) and his sons Petruk, Gareng, and Bagong, the servant clowns or *panakawan* of *wayang kulit*. (Photograph author)

in *wayang kulit* and other classical forms of Javanese theatre.

The *wayang kulit* puppets are opaque, and on the screen they are seen as dark shadows articulated by precise lace-like perforations. The screen is divided in two, the right-hand side being reserved for the good characters, and the left for the evil party. This polarity, however, is not rigid, since both parties include characters with qualities that could belong to the opposing one. At the sides of the 4-metre-long screen the puppets stand in rows with their rods stuck into the soft trunk of a banana tree placed below the screen. When the play begins the *gunungan*, a tapering structure resembling a temple spire, is removed from in front of the screen. The *gunungan* is the symbol of the 'wayang world' and a kind of 'curtain' marking the beginning of the play, changes of scene, and the end. It is also used for special effects such as storms, or even the disruption of the cosmic order. Like all other features of *wayang kulit*, the *gunungan* has many symbolic meanings; it is said to symbolize, for example, the World Mountain, the tree of life, or the cosmic order.

In earlier times it was customary for women and children to watch the play from in front of the screen, while men sat behind it, thus being able to see the orchestra, the *dalang*, and the brightly coloured puppets. This custom is no longer maintained—at least in large-scale public performances—and today the performance can be viewed from both sides of the screen. In its many variants, *wayang kulit* is performed throughout Java on feast days. Performances are regularly staged by the *kraton*, and they are also broadcast frequently.

Shadow theatre still has its traditional, deep, and even sacral meaning, and performing and viewing the play can be experienced as a kind of spiritual exercise called *semadi*.

The steady popularity of *wayang kulit* has also made it a platform of various ideologies. It was used to propagate the Islamic faith, and Western missionaries have also spread the message of Christianity with their Western-influenced puppets (Plate 57). In later years the naturalistic puppets of *wayang Pancasila* (*Pancasila*: the doctrine of the spiritual foundations of the Indonesian Republic) presented to the people the history of Indonesian independence (see Plate 13). The Chinese minority of Java have also developed their own shadow puppets, combining Javanese and Chinese features (see Plate 112). There are also many *wayang kulit*-related drama forms, of which the most archaic is *wayang beber*, now practically extinct. In *wayang beber* the *dalang* illustrated the story by opening a painted scroll supported by two poles. Another now rare form is *wayang klitik*, based on the Islamic Damar Wulan story cycle. It is performed without a screen with flat, wooden puppets carved in relief.

Wayang golek is a still-popular form of rod puppetry, which according to tradition was invented by a Javanese Muslim ruler in the late sixteenth century. Its main repertoire is derived from the Menak cycle, dealing with the Muslim hero Amir Hamzah. Local

57. *Wayang kulit* puppets made by order of Christian missionaries. (Photograph author)

58. A *wayang golek* performance.
(Photograph author)

variants of *wayang golek* have evolved in various parts of Java. The tradition is strongest in West Java, where it has been used in performing the stock repertoire of *wayang purwa*, that is, the *Ramayana*, the *Mahabharata*, local tales, and *The Adventures of Prince Panji*. *Wayang golek* uses a set of 60–70 puppets, which do not always portray specific characters, but stock types, the puppets thus being interchangeable. The heads and arms are carved three-dimensionally in wood, and the lower part of the body is covered by a batik sarong, beneath which the *dalang* operates the rod that makes the puppet's head turn (Plate 58). He uses his other hand to manipulate the rods for the arms and hands. There is no screen, the *dalang*, the orchestra, and the singers all being visible to the audience. Although *wayang golek* is performed in many places, *wayang kulit* is still the most popular form of Javanese puppet theatre. It is the origin of the whole '*wayang* family', and has provided the general aesthetics, characterization, and repertoire of Javanese classical theatre as a whole.

Court Dances: Bedhaya and Serimpi

Many ceremonial court dances developed in the *kraton* of Java. The most valued of these are *bedhaya* and *serimpi*. They are both slow, restrained group dances performed by women to the accompaniment

87

of choral singing and *gamelan* music, and their traditions are especially linked to the *kraton* of Yogyakarta and Surakarta in Central Java. The *bedhaya*, laden with deep symbolic or even religious meaning and usually performed by nine dancers, is along with its many variations the most sacred of all Javanese court dances. Performances and even rehearsals are restricted to certain places and times (Plate 59). It is usually performed at major court festivities, such as coronations or the sultan's birthday.

The oldest existing form is the *bedhaya ketawang*, commemorating the bond between Senapati, the first sultan of Mataram (1584–1601) and the mythical Queen of the Southern Sea. It is still preserved as a *pusaka*, or royal heirloom, in the *kraton* of Surakarta. Along with the three forms of *bedhaya* inherited from the ancient Kingdom of Mataram, there are several other *bedhaya* compositions, most of which were created between the mid-eighteenth century and the middle of the twentieth century. Although the *bedhaya* is basically 'a monopoly of the *kraton*', often created by the sultans themselves, it could also be staged by high officials in its less sacred forms.

The *bedhaya* is an extremely slow and solemn dance. The dancers arrive on the scene in an orderly geometric procession formation carrying the hems of their batik sarongs (Plate 60). Majestic, almost martial, music accompanies them to the scene of the performance,

59. Court dancers rehearsing *bedhaya* in front of the Golden Hall in the *kraton* of Yogyakarta. (Photograph author)

60. Procession of noble *bedhaya* dancers in the *kraton* of Yogyakarta. (Kraton of Yogyakarta)

usually a *pendopo* hall open at the sides—a typical feature of *kraton* architecture (Plate 61). The dancers then kneel down in respect before beginning the actual dance. The footwork is relatively simple, but the grouping of the dancers changes almost unnoticeably, creating ever-newer and increasingly intricate patterns, like pieces on a chessboard. The face is kept strictly expressionless, and the eyes look down, while the dancers undulate to the *gamelan* music in a continuous flow of movement like underwater plants. Indian-derived hand gestures are used, but they no longer have any direct symbolic meaning and have become extremely streamlined and decorative dance gestures. In the basic position, the dancers' knees are bent making the body Z-shaped. This extremely demanding position, sometimes making the dancers collapse and faint, permits, however, flexibility for sharp rises and falls of the body accentuating the otherwise continuous legato-like movement. At times the dancers continue their uninterrupted movement crouching on their knees, and at other times they make sudden, deep asymmetric bends. In the climax the two main dancers separate themselves slightly from the group to begin an extremely stylized battle with their wavy-bladed krises (*keris*: dagger), after which the dancers leave the scene in a procession-like formation similar to their entrance.

The *bedhaya* dancers wear a batik sarong, often decorated with motifs restricted to court use. The upper body is clothed by a tight-fitting dark velvet blouse, and a dance scarf is worn around the

89

61. The great *pendopo* hall at the Mangkunegaran *kraton* in Surakarta. (Photograph author)

waist. This is skilfully manipulated with the tips of the fingers, the controlled handling being an essential part of the choreography. The dancers wear gilt tiaras with large brightly coloured feathers softly following their movements and delicate bends of the head. The dancers' bodies are painted in a golden hue, and the eye make-up corresponds to the old court traditions. In the various genres of *bedhaya*, the even-tempoed music is performed by *gamelan* ensembles, which in the earliest traditions were rather small. The text sung by the chorus usually has no direct connection with the dance or the stylized battle enacted by the principal dancers, but only sets the general mood of the performance.

The *bedhaya* still has a deep religious meaning to both the performers and the spectators. Its aesthetic principles are linked to a non-verbal, esoteric conception of beauty and strength, and the dancing of *bedhaya* is seen as a kind of yoga or meditation. The nine dancers have been explained as symbolizing the eight cardinal points and the centre of the universe—a conception derived from ancient Indian cosmology. The number of dancers can also be seen as representing the nine human orifices, and the whole composition is thus associated with the structure of the human body. Along with other interpretations, the *bedhaya* can also be regarded as a representation of the struggle between the human mind and desires.

The *serimpi*, sometimes called 'the sister of *bedhaya*', shares its basic aesthetics, dance technique, and costumes with the *bedhaya*, although it is performed by only four female dancers (Colour Plate 24).

62. *Golek* performance at Dalem Pujokusuman, Yogyakarta. (Photograph author)

Serimpi is also of ancient origin, with distinct symbolic connotations. Its four dancers are seen as representing the four universal elements of earth, water, fire, and air, as well as the four cardinal points of the universe. The composition depicts a battle with krises between the four heroines, although the actual plot or story is only alluded to, as if taking place in a distant, mythical past. Notwithstanding its ritual nature, *serimpi* does not have quite the same aura of sacredness as *bedhaya*, and when court dances began to be taught outside the *kraton* in the 1910s, *serimpi* was chosen as the basis of Javanese classical female dance.

There are also forms of solo dance cultivated in the *kraton*, which do not, however, have the same ritual connotations as the above-mentioned female group dances. The most popular one is the *golek*, a solo dance portraying a young girl growing into womanhood (Plate 62). The basic position and technique resemble *bedhaya* and *serimpi*, but the descriptive movements depict the self-beautifying of a maiden. The name *golek* refers to *wayang golek* puppetry, and this dance has its parallel in the *wayang golek* repertoire. The *golek* has traditionally been performed at festive receptions, and at present it has become one of the stock numbers of tourist shows.

Martial dances for male performers also evolved in the *kraton*, the most famous group being the *beksa* of the *kraton* of Yogyakarta. They were originally performed by two groups of soldiers of the royal guard, depicting scenes of warfare with a strong military spirit.

Most of the court dances are traditionally attributed to sultans, and many of the rulers are themselves known to have been skilled dancers. The performers were mostly close relatives of the sultan, or members of the court and the bodyguard. The dances are of a highly aristocratic character (Colour Plate 25), and consequently Central Javanese dancers have usually had an exceptionally high social status. In 1918 the first public dance society was founded, extending the court traditions outside the *kraton*. However, the aristocratic nature of the dances has survived despite these developments. At present, the court traditions are taught and performed by several private dance societies, although the *kraton* of Surakarta and especially Yogyakarta are still the best places to see authentic court performances.

Masked Dances: Topeng

Java is the home of several mask theatre and dance traditions, which are commonly referred to as *wayang topeng* (*wayang*: shadow or puppet; *topeng*: mask). They are believed to have evolved from early shamanistic burial and initiation rites. Mask traditions universally contain shamanistic features, for when an actor puts on a mask he gives up his own identity and embodies the character of the mask, usually a mythical being such as a demon, a supernatural hero, or a god. The earliest known literary reference to *wayang topeng* is from 1058, and mask theatre is believed to have been very popular in the kingdoms of East Java over the following centuries. This led to the birth of *wayang wwang*, a spectacular form of court theatre, where some of the characters are believed to have worn masks. Two performing traditions of *wayang topeng* developed: the impressive dance-drama of the court, and the village traditions, which still contain ancient shamanistic elements. Throughout the history of *topeng*, the 'major' court traditions and the 'minor' village traditions have been in a constant state of interaction.

Wayang topeng is often based on the *Mahabharata* and the *Ramayana* epics, among other sources, but from a very early stage *The Adventures of Prince Panji* has been the most popular source of its plot material. This cycle was created in East Java during the Majapahit dynasty. Its hero, the handsome Prince Panji, combines features of earlier historical and mythical figures. He became the Javanese ideal hero *par excellence* along with Arjuna of the *Mahabharata* and Prince Rama of the *Ramayana*. By the end of the fourteenth century, the Panji romance spread to Bali and other parts of South-East Asia, where it is known in several versions. One of these is given below.

Prince Panji is distressed over the mysterious disappearance of his bride Candra Kirana on the eve of their wedding. A princess claiming to be Candra Kirana arrives at his palace, but she does not look at all like her. She is in fact a female demon who has fallen in love with Panji. The false bride says she is Candra Kirana who had to change her appearance when she fell into the hands of the goddess of death, and marrying Panji will restore her former looks. Panji orders preparations to be made for the marriage, and he eagerly awaits to see his beloved again in her familiar shape. Meanwhile, the real Candra Kirana has been taken away to a forest, where she complains of her fate until the gods mercifully tell her that she must return to the palace disguised as a man. She follows these orders, but is not able to contact Prince Panji. However, she sends him a message revealing the true character of the false bride. Then she must flee the palace. The horrified Panji has the demon-bride executed and rushes off to find his beloved. The lovers must, however, experience many adventures before being reunited. Panji lives for a while among ascetics and as a servant in palaces, and meets with many joys and dangers. Candra Kirana, disguised as a man, has her own adventures, and finally becomes the king of Bali. The climax is a battle scene, where Panji and Candra Kirana find themselves both on the same battlefield, but do not recognize each other. When the gods told the maiden to dress as a man, they also told her that she will not meet her lover before she has shed his blood in a duel. Now, the maiden, in the guise of the king of Bali, and Prince Panji engage in combat, but they are so even that neither is wounded. Candra Kirana resorts to feminine means and uses her hairpin, and only then is Panji wounded. They recognize each other, and the story has a happy ending.

Full-length *topeng* performances have become extremely rare, but *topeng* dance numbers are still presented. Popular items of repertoire are the introductory dances of Prince Panji and Princess Candra Kirana, allowing them to display their respective psychological qualities with classical dance patterns. In *topeng* these are usually faster and more expressive than in other forms of Javanese dance-drama. An especially popular number is the so-called *kiprah* dance of the enamoured King Klana (also Klono, Kelana) with his red mask. It most probably evolved from ancient ritual dances, and is known in several versions throughout the island of Java. For example, in the *kraton* of Yogyakarta it survives as the classic *Klana topeng* dance (Colour Plate 26; Plate 63), and on the island of Madura it has its own highly different variants. The dance expresses the yearning of King Klana who has fallen in love with Candra Kirana. He imagines meeting his beloved and enacts with extremely expressive dance movements all the gestures of a vain man in love: he spruces himself up, arranges his hair, dresses in his best clothes, and plans to give a present to the object of his affections who never appears. The dance of King Klana is usually performed in the energetic dance style of a strong male figure, but it also exists in a noble *alus* version, where the character is more refined, though still a desperate lover (Plate 64).

The decreased popularity of mask theatre is usually explained by the spread of Islam. When the Central Javanese Mataram kingdom was divided into two in 1755, it was the *kraton* of Surakarta

63. *Klana topeng* dance at Dalem Pujokusuman, Yogyakarta. (Photograph author)

64. *Topeng* dance of a noble *alus* character performed at the *kraton* of Yogyakarta. (Photograph author)

that inherited the ancient *wayang topeng* tradition of Mataram and its old masks. In Yogyakarta, *wayang wong*, which developed in the late eighteenth century, replaced the spectacular mask theatre performances of the court, but the old mask sets are still revered in the *kraton* as royal *pusaka* heirlooms. Today, in the *kraton* of Surakarta and Yogyakarta, *topeng* is performed from time to time, although mostly as solo numbers. In addition to the rarely performed court *topeng*, popular forms of this genre survive and are performed especially in the villages of western Central Java. East Java and the island of Madura have their own mask theatre traditions, but *topeng* mostly thrives in Sunda in West Java, where Cirebon with its small *kraton* has been the traditional centre of *topeng*. Alongside the court performances, the villages around Cirebon still have their own vital mask traditions.

In all parts of Java the *topeng* masks share an aesthetic based on the iconography of the *wayang kulit* puppets. Carved out of wood, they mainly resemble the faces of the three-dimensional *wayang golek* puppets (Plates 65 and 66). Their stylization is almost abstract, and the oval masks of downward tapering form are usually slightly smaller than a human face. The faces of the noble characters are taut, narrowing towards a delicate chin, and the noses are sharply ridged and pointed. The eyes are elongated, and the mouths are small.

65. Heads of Sundanese *wayang golek* puppets resembling *topeng* masks: (*left*) Gathutkaca, son of Bima; (*right*) Semar, father of the servant clowns. (Collection of Theatre Museum, Helsinki; photograph Hannu Männyoksa)

94

Strong characters, such as King Klana, wear energetic masks with long, upturned noses and wide-open, round eyes. The colour symbolism is the same as in the *wayang golek* puppets: noble characters have white or golden masks, although Prince Panji's mask is usually green. The masks of the strong characters, like King Klana, are usually red. The various local traditions clearly differ in style. In Central Java the masks are almost triangular; the masks of Madura retain their own archaic stylization; and the masks of Cirebon are perhaps the most abstract with almost symbol-like faces. The mask sets and collections on display in the National Museum in Jakarta, the Museum of Yogyakarta, and in many *kraton* museums demonstrate not only the local variations of mask styles but also their excellent artistic level.

66. Sundanese *topeng* masks in the collection of the Mangkunegaran *kraton* in Surakarta. (Photograph author)

Court Dance-drama: Wayang Wong

In its grandeur and extreme stylization, the Javanese *wayang wong* (*wayang*: shadow or puppet; *wong*: man) is undoubtedly one of the world's greatest theatrical traditions. Several forms of large-scale dance-drama are known from the early periods of Javanese history. A literary source from AD 930 refers to the *wayang wwang* dance-drama, a kind of *wayang kulit* performance where the puppets were replaced by human dancers. Its dance style is assumed to have been strongly influenced by India, and the actors were masked or unmasked according to the character portrayed. In the Majapahit kingdom, the court dance-drama was called *raket*. The stories were derived from a contemporary East Javanese story cycle known as *The Adventures of Prince Panji*, and the performances are known to have lasted from evening until noon the next day. The theatrical tradition of Hinduized East Java disappeared or partly changed with the spread of Islam to Java in the fourteenth and fifteenth centuries. It was, however, adopted by the Hindu courts of Bali, where it evolved into the *gambuh*, the quintessentially classical style of Balinese dance-drama.

In Java, *wayang topeng* mask theatre remained the most popular form of dance-drama until the eighteenth century. When the kingdom of Mataram in Central Java split in two in 1755 as a result of Dutch domination, the courts of Yogyakarta and Surakarta became rivals—mainly in the field of arts—as the Dutch had considerably curbed the actual political power of the rulers. The court of Surakarta inherited the highly valued *bedhaya* dance and the *topeng* mask theatre from the Mataram kingdom. The Sultan of Yogyakarta, Hamengkubuwana I (1755–92) therefore began to design a new form of theatre as his *pusaka* heirloom. In creating the spectacular *wayang wong* dance-drama, he explicitly strove to revive the dance-drama tradition of the ancient Majapahit dynasty in order to emphasize his role as the true descendant of Majapahit.

Wayang wong has many features in common with the *wayang kulit* shadow theatre. These include a similar overall aesthetic and the same narrative material, mainly from the *Mahabharata* and the *Ramayana* (Colour Plate 27; Plate 67); even the movements of the actors clearly imitate puppets. The steps and gestures of the actors are basically 'two-dimensional', designed to move to the left and the right like the movements of puppets on the screen. Like *wayang kulit*, *wayang wong* is accompanied by a large-scale court *gamelan* orchestra.

Wayang wong was closely linked to court ceremonies. Large spectacles were staged, for example, in honour of the sultan's coronation, or for weddings and birthdays. The performances had a deep symbolic meaning, and the hour of the spectacle and its plots were determined by the fact that the Sultan of Yogyakarta was identified with the Hindu god Vishnu. The performance began early in the morning, when the sun—identified with Vishnu—appeared in the sky. The sultan sat on a holy throne, always facing east in the middle

67. Arjuna on his way searching for Pregiwi and Pregiwati. The static poses and overall aethestics of *wayang wong* are adapted from *wayang kulit*. (VIDOC, Department of the Royal Tropical Institute, Amsterdam, The Netherlands)

of the famous Golden Hall under the highest point of its pyramidical roof, symbolizing the axis of the universe. The performance took place on a lower level in a smaller hall annexed to the magnificent Golden Hall, for no one was permitted to stand higher than the divine sultan. The performances, which lasted two days, were grandiose events, and the audience included not only members of the court but invited colonial representatives as well. *Wayang wong* was an exceptionally expensive art form placing heavy demands on the *kraton*'s treasury. In some cases, the sultan even had to borrow money from the Dutch in order to be able to arrange these spectacles. The last full-scale court performance was staged in 1939.

In Yogyakarta, all the *wayang wong* actors were originally men, and included members of the royal family, other members of the court, and bodyguards. In Surakarta, Pangeran Adipati Mangkunegaran I, the contemporary and rival of Hamengkubuwana I, the creator of *wayang wong*, also began to compose *wayang wong* plays. This marked the beginning of the Surakartan *wayang wong* tradition of the Mangkunegaran *kraton* (Plate 68). The Yogyakartan and Surakartan styles differ in certain respects. In Surakarta women played female roles from the very beginning, and often noble hero characters as well. With its undulating movements, the Surakartan dance style is more subdued than the Yogyakartan style. There are also differences in costume and in the *gamelan* accompaniment.

97

68. Noble Prince Panji with his attendants in a *wayang wong* performance at the Mangkunegaran *kraton* in Surakarta. (VIDOC, Department of the Royal Tropical Institute, Amsterdam, The Netherlands)

The movements of the *wayang wong* dancer-actors are generally fluid and solemn, and recitation is extremely stylized. The main language of the performances is Old Javanese, not the modern language, and the actors recite the lines themselves, while singers sitting among the *gamelan* perform the more demanding vocal parts. The performance is thus an intricately complex whole, where the concept of time and the structure is dictated by the *gamelan*'s soft and elaborate fabric of sound, further elaborated by the recitation, songs, and comments of the chorus. The dancer-actors move slowly, apparently according to their own logic, and from time to time remain frozen, reciting their lines in highly ornamental positions between their elegant dance movements. Because *wayang wong* borrowed the characterization of shadow theatre, the style of dance, costumes, make-up, and vocal technique are all dictated by the stock types portrayed.

The characters fall into three major categories: the female type, the refined male *alus* type, and the strong male *gagah* type. The

69. Sita and her attendant in a typically feminine pose in a *wayang wong* performance at Dalem Pujokusuman, Yogyakarta. (Photograph author)

dancer's physique determines his or her role type. The women must be petite and slender, and they should also have beautiful facial features. The noble male characters must also be slender and delicate, whereas the strong male type should be powerful in both body and appearance. The slow female dance is restrained and graceful, and its movements are directed to a low level covering only a narrow space. The female dancer rarely lifts her feet from the floor, and the basic position is always a demi-*plié* bent slightly forward (Plate 69). The movements of the refined male type are also directed to a rather low level, but the dancers are allowed to lift their feet slightly. Their whole dance technique aims at creating an overall impression of withheld strength, so typical of the South-East Asian hero ideal. The strong male type, on the other hand, moves energetically, standing in a very open leg position and lifting his arms and legs horizontally to create the impression of almost aggressive masculinity (Colour Plate 28; Plate 70; Figure 3). All the role types use four basic hand gestures (Plates 71–74), derived

99

70. The demon-king Ravana
personifying aggressive masculinity
in a *wayang wong* performance at
Dalem Pujokusuman,
Yogyakarta.(Photograph author)

Fig. 3
Four of the basic poses for a strong male
character in *wayang wong*, Yogyakartan
style. (Päivi Lempinen)

100

from the shadow puppets. These, in turn, are partly based on the Indian-influenced dance of the Central Javanese period, as shown by preserved reliefs and sculptures. Unlike the Indian *mudra*, the *wayang wong* hand gestures do not have—at least any more—any direct symbolic meaning. They are rather unforced, albeit extremely decorative gestural extensions of the dance movements.

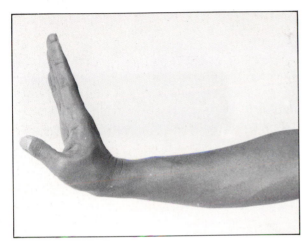

71. First basic hand gesture of *wayang wong*. (Photograph author)

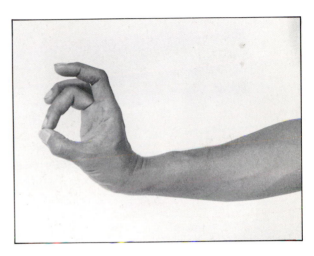

72. Second basic hand gesture of *wayang wong*. (Photograph author)

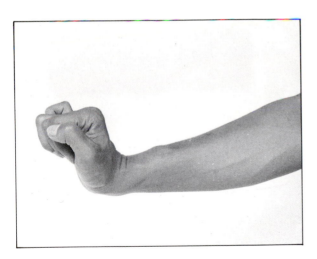

73. Third basic hand gesture of *wayang wong*. (Photograph author)

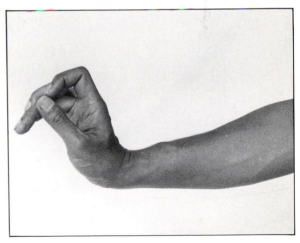

74. Fourth basic hand gesture of *wayang wong*. (Photograph author)

The above three major role types are each divided into a number of subtypes (humble, refined, proud, servant, adviser, etc.). There is a total of twenty-one role types, each with its own style of make-up and dress. The leading types have their characteristic movement patterns revealing their psychological qualities. For example, symmetrical movements indicate strength, stability, and above all humility, whereas asymmetry is a sign of proud and powerful energy. The costume includes a brownish-black batik sarong with a tight black velvet bodice for women, while the men dance with bare torsos. Also worn are jewellery and a crown or tiara, skilfully cut and chased in gilt leather, with the model of the head-dress revealing the rank of the character. The overall aesthetics are familiar to *wayang kulit*, and in this century the dance costume and head-dress were made to correspond more closely to those of shadow puppets. Characterization is further emphasized with facial make-up, as masks are worn only by the demon and monkey figures (Plate 75). The slightly stylized make-up is light for the noble male and female roles, and red for the strong and coarse types. The facial make-up of the *panakawan* or servant clowns is usually white (Plate 76). Make-up can be divided into seven basic types, including, for example, various models of painted whiskers and beards for the men. The actors paint their whole body with yellowish *boreh* liquid, giving the skin a soft golden glow.

75. Hanuman wearing a papier mâché mask in a *wayang wong* performance at Dalem Pujokusuman, Yogyakarta. (Photograph author)

76. The white-faced Semar in a *wayang wong* performance at the *kraton* of Yogyakarta. (Photograph author)

The traditional *wayang wong* plots or *lakon*, which in the early nineteenth century finally developed into written 'librettos', are mostly based on the *Mahabharata* and the *Ramayana*. In Java, these originally Indian epics are regarded as national literature, even to the extent that their heroes are felt to be the mythical ancestors of the Javanese. It is no wonder then that the heroes have, in a way, begun to live their own lives and have given rise to new and purely Javanese stories which no longer have anything to do with the original epic context. For example, the *lakon Rama Nitis* (The Incarnation of Rama) portrays an incarnation of Prince Rama of the *Ramayana* as the god Krishna of the *Mahabharata*. One of the earliest fantasies of this kind is the *kakawin* court poem, *Arjuna Vivaha*, composed in honour of King Airlangga's wedding in 1035, whose principal hero is the virtuous Arjuna of the *Mahabharata*. Although originally official court poetry lauding the virtues of a ruler celebrating his marriage, it has survived as one of the most beloved and valued *lakon* of *wayang wong*.

In *Arjuna Vivaha*, the heavenly realm of the god Indra is in a state of turmoil. A terrifying demon, who is possessed by his love for the nymph Supraba, becomes enraged when Indra refuses to give the maiden to him. A difficult situation arises, for none of the gods can beat the demon in battle, and it is known that only a heroic mortal can do this. A message arrives at a meeting of the gods, telling the assembly that the heroic Arjuna has retired to a cave to practise asceticism and meditation to prepare himself for battle. Indra decides to test Arjuna's will-power and self-control to find out whether he is able to conquer the demon. He selects the seven most beautiful nymphs and sends them to the cave to tempt Arjuna. The loveliest nymph is Supraba, with whom the demon falls in love. To their dismay, the nymphs must return to Indra's heaven, as the fair Arjuna remained unperturbed; he did not even notice the maidens. Indra decides on another trial to find out if Arjuna's asceticism is meant only for his own salvation, or whether he is interested in the most important task of all—to help the whole of creation. Disguised as an old ascetic, Indra finally makes Arjuna speak. To his pleasure, Indra hears that Arjuna is practising meditation in order to better fulfil his duties as a warrior and to be able to help others. The demons hear of Arjuna's meditation, which makes them concerned. One of the demons transforms himself into an enormous wild boar and begins to topple the mountain where Arjuna is meditating in the cave. Bow in hand, Arjuna steps out of the cave, and at the same moment the god Shiva appears in the guise of a king on a hunting expedition, also ready to shoot the boar. They tense their bows at the same time and their arrows fly into the boar's flesh. They meet their mark simultaneously in exactly the same spot, and miraculously blend into a single arrow. Shiva claims the arrow for himself, which leads to an argument and a fight, but Arjuna manages to throw Shiva down on the ground. When he tries to catch Shiva's foot, it miraculously disappears, and flowers begin to rain from heaven as Shiva now appears in his divine form. Arjuna kneels in respect, and the god gives him the magic arrow, instructing him in the art of combat (Plate 77). The time is now ripe for the grand battle, and the gods invite Arjuna to visit them to work out a scheme to find out the demon's weak point. Together with the lovely Supraba, Arjuna, now invisible, sets out to meet the demon, who is overjoyed to see the maiden coming voluntarily to him. The lovesick demon approaches the maiden, but Supraba asks him to reveal the secret of his strength as her bridal reward. The foolish demon reveals that his tongue is the only part of his body that can be wounded. The invisible Arjuna causes a commotion, Supraba flees, and the demon realizes his grave error. An enraged army of demons sets out to attack the heavens. One after another, the heavens fall to the invaders, who now approach Indra's realm, the highest heaven of all. Finally, Arjuna engages the demon in a duel and pretends to be wounded. When the demon begins to boast of his victory, Arjuna suddenly shoots his magic arrow into the demon's tongue, thus defeating him. A great celebration is held in Indra's heaven, and Arjuna is crowned King of Heaven for seven days. He is sprinkled with the water of life, and Supraba, together with the six other nymphs, who tempted

77. God Shiva instructs Arjuna in the art of combat, a modernized version of Surakartan-style *Arjuna Vivaha* performed at Taman Ismail Marzuki, Jakarta. (Photograph author)

him in the cave, are given to him as consorts. After the celebration, however, Arjuna asks Indra to let him return to earth to his brothers. Permission is granted and the seven nymphs express their heartache.

The flourishing period of dance and theatre, which began in the *kraton* of Yogyakarta and Surakarta in the mid-eighteenth century, continued throughout the following century. It led to new forms of *wayang wong*-related dance-drama. The best known of these are *langen driya* and *langen mandra wanara*. Around the middle of the nineteenth century Mangkunegoro V from the Mangkunegaran *kraton* in Surakarta created the *langen driya*, based on the adventures of the hero Darmawula, a story cycle dating back to the East Javanese Majapahit dynasty. It is performed by an all-female cast, who—unlike in *wayang wong*—sing all of their lines. *Langen mandra wanara*, also a kind of *wayang wong*-derived 'dance opera', was created in the late nineteenth century by Prince Danuredjo VII of Yogyakarta. Its plot material is based solely on the *Ramayana*, and its name derives from the epic's monkey characters (*wanara*: monkey). The monkeys also lend a special feature to the whole performing technique—*langen mandra wanara* is performed in a crouching position and the movement patterns are characterized by monkey-like movements and gestures. At present, both *langen driya* and *langen mandra wanara* are rarely performed, although the latter experienced a kind of renaissance in the 1980s when a complete performance was recorded by Radio France. The original *wayang wong*, on the other hand, is still performed actively, and it can be truly regarded as the classical dance-drama of Java. It has evolved into new variants in the twentieth century, which has in many ways been a period of drastic change in the traditional performing arts.

The Twentieth Century

Until the beginning of the twentieth century most of Java's traditions of classical dance and theatre had been closely guarded treasures of the courts. Dance was mainly intended for court rituals, and its training was basically a means of educating the aristocracy and the court. The early years of this century brought about a number of changes that have come to be called the 'democratization of dance'. In 1918 the first dance society, Kridha Beka Wirama, was founded in Yogyakarta to teach court dances to all regardless of class. The idea was launched by the son of the Sultan of Yogyakarta, and the teachers included the best dance masters of the *kraton*. This marked the beginning of a still-active custom whereby the court traditions of Yogyakarta are taught in private dance societies to all who are interested, often for only a nominal fee. At present, the societies receive part of their income from performances aimed mainly at tourists. The leading dance societies in Yogyakarta that actively stage performances are the *kraton*-related Dalem Pujokusuman and Dalem Notoprajan associations.

The gradual popularization of *wayang wong* began in Surakarta in the 1890s when a Chinese businessman founded a commercial group adapting the *wayang wong* tradition of the Mankunegaran *kraton*. This new style, generally referred to as *wayang orang*, was aimed at ordinary city audiences. The company, now under the name of Sriwedari, still performs in the amusement park in Surakarta (Colour Plates 29–31). The Bharata Theatre, founded in the 1940s, maintains the Mankunegaran tradition in this modernized form in Jakarta. *Wayang orang* is usually performed on a Western-type proscenium stage with heavy illusionistic backdrops, and an abundance of various stage effects. Commercial *wayang orang* groups are also active in the smaller towns, such as Semarang and Malang.

Despite modernization, *wayang orang* has preserved something of its original stylized dance-drama character. This is not the case with the Central Javanese *ketoprak* (Plate 78) and the East Javanese *ludruk*, which are forms of popular theatre developed around the end of the nineteenth century. Their plots are based not only on the traditional stock stories from the *Ramayana* and the *Mahabharata* but also on historical or modern topics. The performances are accompanied by music and include dance numbers, although the main emphasis is on a less stylized acting resembling Western spoken theatre. On the whole, stagecraft is similar to *wayang orang*, although there is even more of an emphasis on realism and even naturalism. *Ketoprak*

78. *Ketoprak* performed in the Bharata Theatre, Jakarta. (Photograph author)

and *ludruk* are actively performed on temporary stages and in the theatre halls of amusement parks in various parts of Java.

Since the early nineteenth century, theatre has also been a platform of nationalistic ideas, and in the 1940s, when Indonesia was in the process of gaining independence, even *wayang kulit*, the most traditional form of theatre, was used to propagate patriotism and new political ideas. In the field of dance the new, nationalistic theatre organizations followed the model of the European socialist countries in transforming old traditions into new, 'mass-oriented' variants, such as the peasant's dance, the tea-picker's dance, and the dance of the fishermen. These works are clearly linked to the political ideas of their day, and it is no wonder that they have not found their place in the basic repertoire of Javanese dance. Western theatre and dance has begun to interest Indonesians to an increasing degree, and many artists have studied in the West, especially in the United States since the 1960s. This, of course, had an effect on the development of dance and theatre. Modern Western dance and spoken theatre, and their adaptation to local conditions found a ready response especially among university intellectuals.

In the early 1960s *sendratari* (*seni*: drama, *tari*: dance) was developed as yet another spectacular form of *wayang wong*-derived dance-drama (Colour Plate 32; Plate 79). It had none of the patriotic fervour of the 1940s and 1950s, and was mainly intended for both Javanese and foreign tourists. The first *sendratari* performance was staged in 1961 and was especially designed for an outdoor stage

79. Rama, Sita, and the court in a *sendratari* performance in front of the Prambanan temple in Central Java. (Photograph author)

107

erected in front of the Hindu temple of Prambanan in Central Java with the temple's enormous silhouette as its background. The choice of the theme and venue of this first *sendratari* production is self-evident: the Prambanan temple area is one of Java's main tourist attractions and it is also related to the *Ramayana* through its magnificent series of reliefs. The Prambanan spectacle has come to be known as the 'Ramayana Ballet'. This is indeed an apt name for a genre where the overall dramaturgy with its impressive mass scenes and modern stage techniques is modelled after the practice of Western fairy-tale ballet. The 'Ramayana Festival' is still a yearly event, performed at the time of the full moon from May to October. The scenes and events of the epic are divided into four full-evening performances. *The Abduction of Sita* is presented on the first night, followed by *Hanuman's Mission to Lanka*, *The Conquest of Lanka*, and finally the fall of Ravana and the proof of Sita's marital fidelity.

The *sendratari* of Prambanan turned out to be a success, perhaps partly because of the growing tourist industry focusing on Central Java. It has become an obligatory event for tour groups, and the previous modest stage has been replaced by a luxurious amphitheatre. The 'Ramayana Ballet' served as a model for later *sendratari* productions, which were staged in other parts of Java at sites of touristic interest. While the Prambanan ballet was mostly based on the Central Javanese heritage, the stories and dance styles of later innovations are based on their respective local traditions. Near Surabaya in East Java there is a huge open-air stage with a perfectly conical volcano in the background. It was especially built for a *sendratari* production based on an East Javanese story combining in its presentation East Javanese and Balinese elements. In Cirebon in West Java, the local *sendratari* is staged in front of an ancient stone garden, and its dance style is based on local *topeng* dances. As a kind of Pan-Indonesian state art, the *sendratari* has also been adopted outside Java, for example, in Bali.

The present teaching of dance and drama is organized along Western lines in government-sponsored institutes such as the university-level Institut Seni Indonesia (Indonesian Institute of Arts) in Yogyakarta and in colleges and high schools in various parts of Java. The curriculum includes local traditions as well as Western dance and drama. In Jakarta, the Taman Ismail Marzuki Art Centre is the dominating institute, having played a decisive role in the formation of contemporary Indonesian dance and theatre. The old court traditions live on in the *kraton* of Yogyakarta and Surakarta, within limited resources, and their heritage is also maintained by many private dance societies.

23. Javanese *wayang kulit* shadow puppets. (Collection of Mr A. S. Härö; photograph Hannu Männynoksa)

24. Stylized battle; a *serimpi* dance at the *kraton* of Yogyakarta. (Photograph author)

25. The battle between two princesses; a *golek*-style duo dance of Yogyakartan tradition at Dalem Pujokusuman. (Photograph author)

26. King Klana wearing a non-typical golden mask; a *Klana topeng* dance of Yogyakartan tradition at Dalem Notoprajan. (Photograph author)

27. A scene from the *Ramayana*; a *wayang wong* performance in Yogyakartan style at Dalem Pujokusuman. (Photograph author)

28. Dance of a strong male character; a *wayang wong* solo in Yogyakartan style at the *kraton* of Yogyakarta. (Photograph author)

29.   A scene from a *wayang orang* performance at the Sriwedari Theatre, Surakarta. (Photograph author)

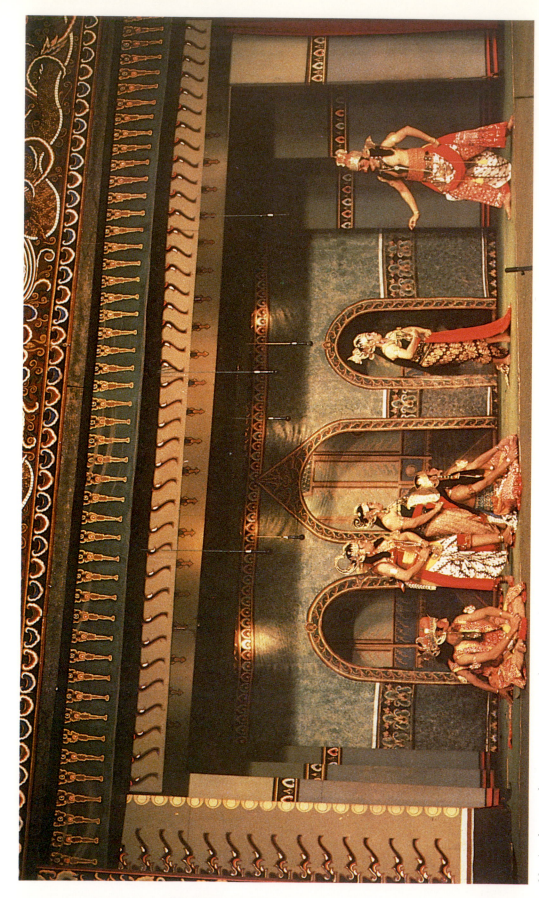

30. Another scene from a *wayang orang* performance at the Sriwedari Theatre, Surakarta. (Photograph author)

31. Semar (*right*) and his sons, the servant clowns of Javanese theatre, in a *wayang orang* performance at the Sriwedari Theatre, Surakarta. (Photograph author)

32. Rama's dance in the Prambanan's *sendratari* performance. (Photograph Fredrik Lagus)

33. Secular *baris* dance, depicting the rapidly changing ▶ moods of a warrior. (Photograph Sakari Viika)

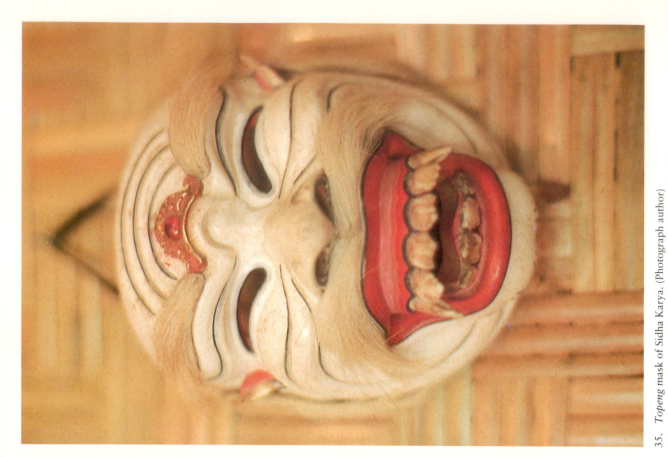

35. *Topeng* mask of Sidha Karya. (Photograph author)

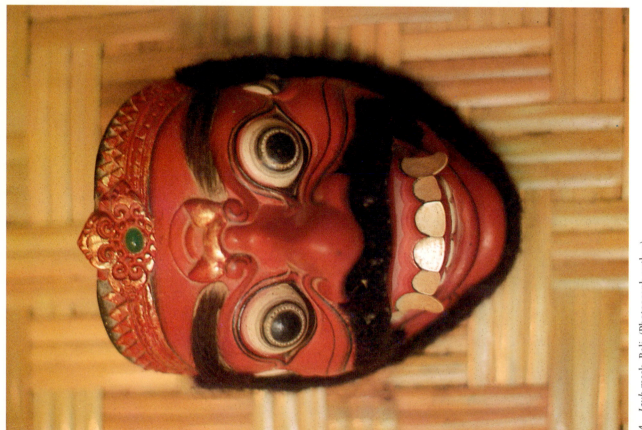

34. *Jauk* mask, Bali. (Photograph author)

36. Barong. (Photograph Robert Wihtol)

37.   The self-stabbing kris dance in a *Barong* performance. (Photograph author)

38.   A young Cambodian dancer, being instructed by her grandmother in the role of a heavenly nymph in Phnom
Penh, wearing a crown inspired by the ancient Khmer reliefs. (Photograph Eero Kukkola)

39. *Ayak-ayak*, a traditional
court dance from the east
coast of the Malay Peninsula.
(Photograph author)

40. A Vietnamese opera actor.
(Photograph Ari Huhtala)

5   Indonesia: Bali

THOUGH only a small island among the thousands of islands forming Indonesia, Bali is a chapter apart in the field of theatre. Despite the strong influence of increasing tourism since the 1930s, its theatrical tradition is one of the most interesting ones in the world. Bali has been the home of several theatrical genres for several centuries. For over half a century, many of the old court theatre traditions have been maintained by village communities. As a result, the classical tradition has been freely interpreted by South-East Asian standards, which have mainly been dominated by the courts. While being preserved, traditions have also been developed, combined, and renewed. Many villages have their own specific traditions of music, theatre, and dance, and performances can be seen daily.

Ancient megalithic ritual sites bear witness to the long history of this island, although they have been covered over by later terraced rice fields and villages. Archaeological finds include bronze artefacts from before the present era. A large bronze drum or kettle gong called 'The Moon of Pejeng', stored in a temple in the small village of Pejeng, indicates later contacts with the Dong-son bronze culture which spread from Southern China to South-East Asia in the first millennium BC. In the eighth and ninth centuries Bali gradually came under the strong influence of an Indianized Hindu–Buddhist culture. Bali was also influenced from time to time by Chinese culture, as can be seen in architecture and the visual arts, and in theatre, where certain mask types and plots indicate Chinese influences.

The nearby island of Java played a decisive role in the development of Balinese culture. Java often overran its tiny neighbour, and Bali did not have its own king until the tenth century. In the late tenth century a Balinese prince married a princess from East Java, which led to a brief union of the kingdoms of Bali and East Java. Around the middle of the fourteenth century the powerful Majapahit dynasty (1293–c.1520), the last Hindu dynasty of Java, conquered Bali, which was to become the place where the old Javanese culture made its greatest impact outside Java itself. The island, however, was never wholly Javanized; it continued to develop its own type of Hinduized culture, which, unlike in Java, managed to retain its integrity against the spread of Islam, which came to dominate Javanese culture in the fourteenth century.

When the East Javanese Majapahit dynasty was conquered by later Islamic dynasties in the early 1500s, members of the Hindu nobility, artists, and priests fled to Bali, bringing with them a new wave of Javanese culture. The culture of the small Balinese kingdoms preserved many features inherited from East Java, whose influence is especially obvious in the oldest preserved forms of Balinese court theatre. Contacts with Islamic Java were few, and Balinese culture was able to develop its intrinsic features undisturbed by outside influences. The West became interested in Bali in the sixteenth century, but the first European trading station was not established until the middle of the nineteenth century. The Dutch soon exerted their influence on the island, but Bali never became a centre of colonial rule in the same way as the island of Java. Balinese culture preserved its original features throughout the nineteenth century, a critical period for many Asian countries under Western colonial rule.

In 1906 the Dutch nevertheless took Bali by force, and most of the members of the eight royal families took their lives in an act of ritual suicide (*puputan*). Only a few of the children of these families survived, though they lost most of their political power and wealth. As a result, the artistic traditions of the courts came to be preserved by the artists now employed by the village communities. The villages of Bali had traditionally maintained a relatively broad degree of self-government with village councils (*banjar*) presiding over common affairs. The musical instruments, masks, and theatrical costumes of the courts, as well as their traditions of theatre and dance, became the cultural heritage of the villages and their councils.

The Western myth of Bali was created in the 1920s and 1930s, and its fame as 'the last South Sea paradise' quickly spread to the West, partly as the result of a regular shipping route opened by the Dutch. Bali soon became a Mecca for artists and travellers thirsting for the exotic. Western artists and intellectuals found their way to Bali, and local artists inspired by Western aesthetics began to develop modern Balinese art. Western travellers and influences soon had an effect on the development of theatre and dance. Luxury hotels began to stage performances which were the predecessors of today's tourist shows, and Balinese dance and theatre became known in the West when a Balinese *gamelan* orchestra and dance troupe toured Europe, performing to enthusiastic audiences.

World War II disrupted the peace of this island paradise, and the Japanese Occupation was a trying time for the Balinese. Indonesia declared its independence on 17 August 1945, and soon afterwards local officials were entrusted with the civilian administration of the island. This ensured the preservation of the island's own culture and religion in predominantly Islamic Indonesia. Further trouble, however, lay ahead. In 1946 the Dutch returned to Bali, which led to a bloody civil war and the heroic *puputan* ritual suicide of Balinese freedom fighters. In the 1960s the island's main volcano, the sacred Gunung Agung, erupted causing great damage and famine.

The beginning of mass tourism was heralded by the opening of an international airport in the late 1960s. The tourist industry has grown steadily, and the present yearly number of visitors is over a million. This has had both positive and negative effects on Balinese theatre and dance. While tourism provides welcomed revenue, it can also erode the standards of performances when local repertoire is adapted to foreign tastes.

Of all the forms of dance and theatre now performed in Bali, the oldest ritual performances predate the arrival of Hindu–Buddhist culture. The Balinese divide their performances into various classes according to their degree of sacredness. The most sacred ones are the *wali* performances, excluded from non-Balinese and outcasts, and are usually held in the most sacred precincts of the temples, which consist of several adjacent courtyards. The *bebali* performances are staged in the outermost temple courtyards, and they are often of an artistic character and open also to foreigners. Other types include magical, though not temple-related, performances, secular performances, and tourist shows. Most of the styles of theatre and dance are performed to the accompaniment of Balinese *gamelan* music. There are many types of *gamelan* music and ensembles in Indonesia, but the *gamelan gong kebyar*, the most popular form of Balinese *gamelan*, is generally faster in tempo and sometimes more feverish and more capriciously accented than the classical *gamelan* of Java. Most of the forms of theatre rely on classical Balinese dance techniques, which partly reiterate old Javanese prototypes which have developed further into a rich, expressive, and dynamic style specific to Bali. Although Balinese theatre is open to new influences, its sacral core appears to have remained unchanged over the centuries.

Ritual Performances: Possession and Trance

Bali is the home of many ritual performances that do not exactly correspond to the traditional Western conceptions of 'theatre' or 'dance'. They are mostly religious rituals, full of magical meaning to their performers and spectators. They may include dances and elements typical of theatrical performances, but are rarely intended for aesthetic pleasure in the present-day Western sense of the term. In these rituals, dance and theatre are always made to serve religious and magical purposes. They are usually performed in the inner temple courtyards in connection with calendar feasts. The performers are mostly non-professional, although some forms of *wali* employ professional dancer-actors. In general, dancing skill is of secondary importance. Ritual performances fall into roughly two groups: ceremonial dances, generally ancient sacred dances of indigenous origin, and trance rituals in which the performers and sometimes the audience as well fall into a trance.

The most sacred dances are seen as an act of worship or a sign of devotion. Because of their nature they can be performed only in the most sacred part of the temple. Most of the *wali* dances are believed to derive from purely indigenous traditions, although they have later borrowed the vocabulary of Hindu–Javanese classical dance. As the most sacred dances are not meant to be performed publicly, it is quite understandable that they have led to secularized variants for commercial purposes.

One of the main groups of *wali* dances is the dignified and ceremonial *baris gede*, performed by men (Plate 80). It is a kind of battle dance, performed by a group arrayed in line, usually with six to sixty dancers. The main emphasis is on co-ordinated group action, sometimes creating the impression of a stylized battle with movements limited to simple steps and leg movements. The dancers, who can be regarded as the bodyguard of deities visiting the temple, wear pyramidical head-dresses decorated with triangular pieces of mother-of-pearl, and in their hands they hold sacred heirloom weapons. The various genres of *baris* are classified according to the types of weapons used. There is also a modern, completely secular variant of the dance.

The secular *baris* is a virtuoso solo in which the dancer portrays the emotions of a warrior departing for the battlefield (Colour Plate 33). The technique is a combination of the sacred *baris* and various elements of Balinese classical male dance (Figure 4). Fast,

80. A variant of the sacred *baris gedé*. (*Theatre Arts Monthly*, August 1936; photograph Rose Covarrubias)

Fig. 4
Movements of the secular *baris*, drawn by Miguel Covarrubias. (*Theatre Arts Monthly*, August 1936)

jerking movements, tensed arm gestures, and expressive eye movements are used to convey the warrior's rapidly changing moods, ranging from courage to fear and from doubt to determination. This form of the *baris* is usually included in dance performances staged for tourists.

Another significant form of the sacred *wali* dance is the *rejang*, a professional group dance, performed by women. Its choreography is based on simple line formations, and it is performed in daytime usually by a group of forty to sixty non-professional dancers. The *rejang* is a relatively simple dance, although its slow movements evoke a dignified feeling of beauty. The *gabor* is another female group dance, a graceful offering-ritual usually performed by professionals, and it is thus natural that its movements do not greatly differ from classical dance. A secular variant of the *gabor* has become established as a general welcoming dance which is usually performed as an opening number in tourist shows or in receiving honoured guests (Plate 81). The original *wali* category includes forms of dance-drama of larger scale as well. These include the *berutuk*, performed by youths in the ancient village of Trunyan. The boys are dressed in banana

81. Popular welcoming dance; a secular variant of the sacred offering-ritual. (Photograph Sakari Viika)

leaves and wear very archaic or even primitive wooden masks, coloured red for male and white for female characters. The whole event contains elements of a social game and a sacred possession ritual.

Bali is famous for its many traditions of trance rituals, where one or several dancers fall into a trance by means of incense, music, chants, prayers, and sometimes drugs. The trance is an altered state of consciousness, and sometimes the audience can also come into contact with the spirit world and be possessed by gods, animistic spirits, or even animal spirits. Trance rituals are not limited to Bali alone. As pointed out above, trance is an integral feature of various ethnic rituals in the so-called shamanistic zone, extending from Korea to Scandinavia. Almost everywhere in Asia, trance, in one form or another, is an integral part of indigenous ritual theatre. In view of its small size, there are exceptionally many kinds of trance rituals in Bali.

Sang Hyang (*Sang*: Lord; *Hyang*: God) is a genre of trance dances generally performed in remote villages, although occasional tourist performances can also be seen. It comprises several forms, and local variants abound in many villages. In most types of *Sang Hyang* the men become possessed by animal spirits. In *Sang Hyang jaran* the men are transformed into horses, in *Sang Hyang lelipi* they are changed into snakes, and in *Sang Hyang celeng* they are possessed by the spirits of pigs. The performances have the purpose of ritual purification; for example, men in the pig trance 'eat dirt'—at least symbolically—and thus aid in the purification of their community. Trance rituals often become hectic events, where the village priests and their attendants control unpredictable action to avoid injuries. After the performance the priests sprinkle the participants with holy water, thus helping them regain normal consciousness.

The most famous and without doubt the most beautiful form of *Sang Hyang* is the *Sang Hyang dedari* (*dedari*: fairy), performed by pre-adolescent girls. The performers are usually temple servants of some kind, sometimes relatives of the priests, but without any professional dance training. The girls are induced into a trance, after which they begin to perform an intricate dance partly based on various ancient animal movements. They are then lifted on to the shoulders of men, who move rapidly, while the girls continue their dance without any support. Finally, the girls dance on glowing coals, and are later brought back to normal consciousness. The young performers are believed to be possessed by celestial nymphs. The almost feverish vocabulary of movement of the *Sang Hyang dedari* has influenced other dance forms such as the classic *legong*.

There are also other Balinese trance rituals, some of which have been combined with less sacred forms of dance-drama. Among the most famous of these is the self-stabbing kris dance (Plate 82) related to the 'Barong–Rangda' performances. Trance rituals have also evolved into purely commercial performances. One of the best known of these variants is the *cak* or *kecak*, which was created in the twentieth century.

82. A kris dancer. (*Theatre Arts Monthly*, August 1936; photograph Rose Covarrubias)

The East Javanese Heritage: Wayang and Gambuh

Surviving in Bali are two genres of theatre—the *wayang kulit* shadow theatre and the *gambuh* court dance-drama—which have preserved the ancient Hindu–Javanese tradition in a possibly more archaic form than any corresponding form of theatre in Java. Between the ninth and the sixteenth centuries Bali had close contacts with East Java, at times belligerent and at times peaceful. Over these centuries,

Bali adopted the Hinduized court culture of East Java and its various forms of theatre.

The Balinese *wayang kulit* is closely related to Javanese shadow theatre. This is indicated by the use of the name *wayang kulit* (*wayang*: shadow, puppet; *kulit*: leather) on both islands. Shadow theatre is believed to have arrived in Bali from Java along with the Hinduized court culture before the eleventh century. At this time the Balinese adopted the *Ramayana* and *Mahabharata* epics of India, which constitute the main repertoire of shadow theatre in both Java and Bali.

The Balinese and Javanese leather puppets are skilfully cut and incised, and they share common aesthetic principles: the puppet's face and feet are shown in profile while the torso is presented frontally. The arms, articulated at the shoulder and the elbow, are the only jointed parts. Javanese and Balinese puppets differ, however, in style. Experts assume that the Javanese puppets received their extreme stylization and symbolic character from the Islamic courts after the fall of the Majapahit empire. The Balinese puppets, on the other hand, reflect older prototypes. This is shown by the fact that the puppets of Bali with their head-dresses, hairstyles, costumes, and their more realistic features reflect the stylization and aesthetics of the low-relief carvings of Majapahit temples in East Java. This archaic puppet style was preserved in Bali when contacts with Islamic Java ceased after the sixteenth century.

In Java *wayang kulit* developed into a large-scale, classical form of theatre of complex philosophical and aesthetic content, which had a decisive effect on the visual arts and other forms of theatre. In Bali shadow theatre also retained its ritual character and its role as a mediator of moral values, but it did not influence other forms of theatre to the same extent as in Java. However, the traditional Balinese style of painting (the so-called *wayang* style) is based on the stylization of the *wayang* puppets.

The *primus motor* of *wayang kulit* is the *dalang* who manipulates the puppets and acts as a narrator. He must have command of a wide range of vocal expression and the movement patterns of various puppets in addition to being responsible for the sacrifices and rituals connected with the performances. *Wayang kulit* can be performed both in the daytime and at night. The night performances are literally a theatre of shadows, as the *dalang* moves the puppets behind a lit screen, while a screen is not used in the daytime form (*wayang lemah*). The Balinese *wayang kulit* does not require as large a troupe as its Javanese counterpart (Plate 83), and the former normally consists of the *dalang* and his assistants, and a small *gamelan* ensemble, usually with four metallophones.

The stories are derived not only from the originally Indian *Ramayana* and *Mahabharata* epics but also from East Javanese story cycles, such as *The Adventures of Prince Panji*, known as *Malat* in Bali, and the *Calonarang*, which deals with magical powers and horrible witches. As in most other classical forms of Balinese theatre,

83. Balinese *wayang kulit* performance. (Photograph author)

the majority of the characters speak Kawi, the language of the Javanese courts from the tenth to the fourteenth century. The servant clown characters speak colloquial Balinese, translating the dialogue for the audience unfamiliar with Kawi. A *wayang* performance is a highly diverse combination of moral teachings, adventure, and slapstick and obscene humour performed by the clowns, much loved by the Balinese. *Wayang kulit* is still popular and several hundred *dalang* are active in Bali.

The *gambuh* is an old form of court dance-drama. It has not been possible to trace its roots, or to define which Javanese traditions constitute its origins. Even the etymology of its name remains unknown. It is known, however, that this genre came from the royal courts of East Java. The *gambuh* tradition is at least four hundred years old, and it has had a great influence on other forms of theatre in Bali and Balinese dance in general. *Gambuh* is performed in the daytime, and it belongs to the semi-sacred *bebali* dances. While originally performed at court festivities, it can be seen at present in temples and in commercial performances, although the latter are very rare.

The *gambuh* repertoire is drawn from classical epic literature, usually East Javanese tales relating to Prince Panji. As in the *wayang*

118

kulit, several languages are used with the royal characters speaking Kawi, the old Javanese court language, and the comic servant characters conversing in colloquial Balinese. The musical accompaniment is extremely complex and perhaps the most demanding form of Balinese music. The orchestra is relatively small and dominated by long, wailing flutes. *Gambuh* was originally performed by an all-male cast, but today women usually play female roles and sometimes even noble heroic characters.

Like most South-East Asian theatre traditions, the *gambuh* has distinct stock characters with specific styles of dance, make-up, and costume. The characters correspond to the Indonesian classification according to which heroes are represented in refined (*alus*) and sweet (*manis*) styles. Ministers, attendants, and evil figures are portrayed in strong (*keras*) and coarse (*kasar*) styles. The general dance style of *gambuh* is characterized by stiff shoulders, tensely moving arms and expressive, upwardly bent movements of the fingers. In the basic position, the thighs and knees are turned outwards, with the legs forming a kind of rhombus, and the shoulders are pulled up so that the head rests on the torso. The dancer often lowers his centre of gravity in a kind of demi *plié* by bending the legs and shifting his weight from one leg to another. The hands repeat the conventional gestures, echoing the distant influence of the *mudra*, the symbolic hand gestures of Indian dance. In fact, the Sanskrit term *mudra* is still used in Balinese to denote a gesture. The facial expression is also dictated by convention, but expressive eye movements are used considerably more than in Javanese dance. This dance technique can well be described as the Balinese classical style, for it has been adapted in the techniques of other major genres such as the *legong*, the *topeng*, and the *arja*.

The court performances originally went on for days, but a modern-day *gambuh* performance lasts only a few hours. It is composed of stock scenes, where fixed characters present monologues, dialogues, dances typical of their roles, and sometimes fighting scenes. Traditionally, sets or props are not used. The performing area, usually a second temple courtyard in the *gambuh* as well as in other *bebali* performances, is fitted with traditional parasols and bamboo decorations, with the costumes, based on old court dress, providing additional visual splendour. A typical *gambuh* costume consists of a long-legged and long-sleeved white undergarment and a wide, gold-embroidered collar with wide gold-patterned strips of fabric hanging down to the knees. The actors move the strips in the same delicate way as the Javanese court dancers handle their long scarves. The costume includes an impressive piece of headgear, often decorated with live flowers. Like the dance technique of the *gambuh*, the costume was also adopted by other traditions of theatre.

The present repertoire represents only a small fraction of the original *gambuh* tradition. When the Dutch conquered the Balinese courts in the early twentieth century, the *gambuh* lost its original royal patronage. In its extreme sophistication, it could not survive as such in the village communities. Performances were shortened and the style was vulgarized, but despite these developments the *gambuh* is still being performed. The Akademi Seni Tari Indonesia (Indonesian Dance Academy), organized along all-Indonesian lines, and other institutions are striving to revive this genre. Several groups specializing in *gambuh* and *gambuh* clubs are active in various parts of Bali, but the standards of their performances vary greatly.

Forms of Mask Theatre: Wayang Wong and Topeng

There are two classic forms of mask theatre in Bali: the *wayang wong* and the *topeng*. Both contain features derived from the old Hindu court culture which was adopted from Java. They developed into their present forms under the patronage of the Balinese courts in the seventeenth and eighteenth centuries, especially in the central court, which was first located in Gelgel and after the beginning of the eighteenth century in Klungkung. Their creation is associated with certain artists and artist families. The oldest mask sets are revered because of their sanctity and like old theatrical costumes they are passed on as family heirlooms.

The *wayang wong* (*wayang*: shadow, puppet; *wong*: man) dance-drama was created when a Balinese king wished to use his old, inherited masks in a new form of theatre based on the *Ramayana*. It was not, however, a completely new invention, being based on already existing forms of theatre such as the *wayang kulit* and the *gambuh*. Certain postures and gestures were adopted from shadow theatre, while *gambuh* provided the style of dance and even complete dance numbers. The *wayang wong* is an impressive, large-scale form of dance theatre, in which decorative, slightly Chinese-influenced masks and large head-dresses offer visual splendour. As in other South-East Asian *Ramayana*-related drama forms, for example, the *khon* of Thailand and the *wayang wong* of Java, the noble heroes and heroines no longer wear masks. They are worn only by actors playing the demon and monkey characters.

Monkeys have a central role in *wayang wong* (Plate 84). In Bali, monkeys have been revered as guardian spirits, and they have been the inspiration for many theatrical creatures, combining simian features with elements of other animals, such as tigers or even birds. The monkeys' pantomime-like gestures add a special flavour to the movements employed in *wayang wong*. Along with the heroes, dancing in the pure classical style, the monkeys introduce positions and gestures based on animal movements adapted from earlier traditions. Despite their apparently relaxed nature, their execution is based on fixed choreographies.

The cast of a *wayang wong* performance includes several dozen dancer-actors. Experienced professionals play roles such as the heroes and the demon-king Ravana, usually employing classical dance techniques, while the monsters and the monkeys are often played by amateurs. A performance usually elaborates only a single episode

84. Balinese *wayang wong* mask of Hanuman. (Photograph author)

of the *Ramayana*. The dialogue and language have been adopted from shadow theatre, though in a simplified form. *Wayang wong* performances still have ritual significance, and many of the masks are regarded as highly sacred objects.

Along with *wayang wong*, the *topeng* is another important form of mask theatre created in the central court of Bali. Here too, the old masks are venerated as sacred heirlooms believed to possess magical powers. *Topeng* can be described as a Balinese chronicle play with plots relating to the island's history, ancient kings, ministers, and court intrigues. There are two types of *topeng*. *Topeng pajegan* (*pajegan*: offering), also known as *topeng wali*, is performed by a single actor as a kind of monodrama which is still regarded as having a profound magical–religious meaning. The performer is at the same time a priest and an actor. In the latter capacity he displays considerable virtuosity, changing his character and movements according to the masks used in the play. The one-man *topeng* is still performed in various rituals, such as the filing of teeth, weddings, and funerals. In the historically younger *topeng panca* five actors appear. In both types, the action consists of a series of stock scenes presented in predictable order.

Balinese *topeng* came about in the seventeenth century, when a new form of dance-drama was created for masks inherited from East Java. The old masks are still revered to such a degree that they are very rarely used and may not be photographed. Over the centuries *topeng* became popular throughout Bali, and new mask sets were made. For dramatic action, the main mask types are the refined (*alus*), white-faced king (*dalem*), his white-faced consort, the strong large-eyed antagonist king, and a number of strong minister characters with face colour ranging from creamy to grey and red (Plates 85–87). A comic touch is added by several grotesque clown masks, often portrayed as suffering from physical defects. The masks of the clowns leave the mouth visible and cover only the upper part of the face,

121

85. *Topeng* mask of the noble king. (Photograph author)

86. *Topeng* mask of the noble queen. (Photograph author)

87. *Topeng* mask of a strong minister. (Photograph author)

88. *Jauk* mask. (Photograph author)

permitting the actors to present their lines. The task of the clowns is to describe the plot to the audience in the vernacular, as several languages are spoken in *topeng*, for example, classical Sanskrit and Kawi.

The masks of *topeng* include those for special characters such as *jauk* (Colour Plate 34; Plate 88) who are not directly related to the dramatic action of a performance. Some of the characters are presented in their own, separate introductory dances. One such character is the white-haired Tua, wearing a light-coloured old man's mask (Plate 89). In the one-man *topeng* the final mask is usually

89. Old man's *topeng* dance.
(Photograph Sakari Viika)

123

90. An actor demonstrating the hand movements of the noble king in *topeng*. (Photograph author)

the smilingly grotesque Sidha Karya (the one who fulfils the task). It is a good example of the typically Balinese way of combining the grotesquely comic with the sacred. The mask of Sidha Karya, with its white face, buck-teeth and almost mad smile, is actually the most sacred of all *topeng* masks (Colour Plate 35). It is only when he wears this mask that the actor may recite the Sanskrit prayers. On the other hand, Sidha Karya may behave in a very unruly manner, and small children in the audience are prepared for his well-meant teasing.

The acting technique concentrates on virtuoso characterization. The language of gesture is mainly based on classic Balinese dance derived from *gambuh*, although it varies greatly according to character (Plate 90). The noble king is always alert, the old man shakes and shudders absent-mindedly, and the red-faced minister with his broad movements represents the universal mood of wonder. In the one-man *topeng pajegan* the dancer sets his mask basket in front of the *gamelan*, from where he chooses and dons the appropriate masks. The presentation of the stock characters thus provides the essence of the actual scenes. With its five actors, *topeng panca*, developed from the one-man *topeng* in the late nineteenth century, has smoothly flowing dramatic action without interruptions. Unlike the sacred *topeng pajegan*, the group *topeng* is a theatrical performance without any ritual significance.

124

The Royal Dance of the Maidens: Legong

Legong is probably the best-known form of contemporary Balinese dance theatre (Plate 91). It is worthy of this reputation, as this form of dance-drama, performed by two or mostly three girls, represents the classical standard of Balinese female dance. *Legong* was created at the turn of the eighteenth century by combining elements from older traditions such as *gambuh* and the *Sang Hyang dedari* trance dance with its many ancient animal movements (Figure 5). Early in its development a variant of *legong* was performed by young boys, but it was rechoreographed for girls by royal command. The pre-adolescent girls were chosen from nearby villages, and they served as *legong* dancers until puberty. Present-day tourist shows may employ adult dancers.

The standard plot of *legong* is based on a cycle of East Javanese tales relating to the adventures of the legendary Prince Panji. *Legong* is, however, an implicitly abstracted form of dance theatre, and the various events are vaguely alluded to. It usually concentrates on only a fragment of the whole tale, where the King of Lasem has

91. *Legong* dancers. (From Jorden Runt, *Magasin för Geografi och Resor*, Stockholm: Natur och Kultur, 1929)

125

Fig. 5
Movements of *legong*, drawn by Miguel Covarrubias. (*Theatre Arts Monthly*, August 1936)

kidnapped Princess Rangka Sari, who has fallen in love with Prince Panji. The king tries to win the heart of the beautiful princess, but she does not respond to his advances. The princess demands that the king beat Panji in battle. The unhappy king goes off to battlefield, but on his way he meets a crow, the bird of ill omen. The king arrogantly strikes the bird with his fan and thus seals his fate in the coming battle with Panji.

One of the dancers plays the princess, another has the role of the king, and a third plays both a servant and the bird. All three dancers wear the same standard costume in which the waist and back are enclosed tightly in a long belt of fabric with a long skirt

92. Teaching the *legong*. (*Theatre Arts Monthly*, August 1936; photograph Rose Covarrubias)

covering the legs. The material of the costumes is typically gold-embroidered dark green or violet fabric, originally derived from court dress. The dancers also have a wide collar of gilt leather and headgear of the same material, which is decorated with fresh flowers. They usually have fans in their hands, and the dancer in the role of the bird has gilt wings. In the original court performances the dancers wore gold ornaments and headgear with jewels.

The dancers do not speak or sing themselves, and the lines are presented by singers among the orchestra. *Legong* is accompanied by an exceptionally old type of sweet-sounding *gamelan*. The dance is based on *gambuh*, but the special features of costume, the tightly wound waist and the narrow lower part, create a different aesthetic for the dance. The legs are bent forward with the torso also leaning forward. Delicate movements of the head and tensed arms are characteristic of *legong*. An aesthetic concept of tropical insects and animals may account for the way in which the dancers' fingers tremble like antennae when they are not handling their fans. The technique also involves the expressive eye movements, typical of Balinese dance but rare elsewhere in South-East Asia.

A *legong* performance begins with a complex introductory dance, followed by the drama proper and an abstract epilogue dance. The movements are fast, sometimes creating geometric floor patterns, and the characters communicate with rapid movements and expressions, ending at times in precise unison. The overall mood is almost feverish. *Legong* dancers begin their training in early childhood. The demanding technique is taught by moving and twisting the girls' arms, necks, and body until 'the dance enters their innermost being', that is, they learn it (Plate 92). Many villages have their own *legong* traditions, and at present the style is used not only for performing *The Adventures of Prince Panji* but for other tales as well.

Magic Drama: Barong, Rangda, and Calonarang

Two mythical beings are ever-present in Bali. They can be seen in travel advertisements and postcards, and their colourful masks are sold everywhere as souvenirs. They are Barong resembling a lion with its long mane (Colour Plate 36; Plate 93), and the witch Rangda with matted hair and large tusks (Plate 94). Both are invested with a strong aura of magic. Old, authentic Barong and Rangda masks with holy inscriptions, consecrated in temple rituals, are kept in village temples, where they are revered as patron spirits (Plate 95). The mythology of Barong and Rangda is complex and anything but unequivocal. They often have leading roles in village events and drama performances, of which the best-known is the *Calonarang*, based on an East Javanese legend.

The term *barong* can refer to a mythological animal mask in general. In practice, however, it usually means Barong, a mythical animal figure known to all Balinese. Inside its hairy body are two male dancers, whose movements and steps must be completely co-ordinated

129

93. Barong having a problem with his
    leg. (Photograph Robert Wihtol)

94. Rangda. (From Jorden Runt,
    Magasin för Geografi och Resor,
    Stockholm, Natur och Kultur,
    1929)

95. Prayers for Barong. (*Theatre Arts Monthly*, August 1936; photograph Rose Covarrubias)

to perform its fast turns and leaps. The forward dancer supports and moves the head and jaws. The decorative, slightly Chinese-influenced Barong mask is stylistically related to the old *wayang wong* masks. The Barong mask has bulging eyes, large ears, and a head-dress of gilt leather and shining pieces of mirror, and large ears. Similarly, the upright tail and the ornaments of the hairy body, made of the same material, glimmer along with the Barong's movements.

The Barong figure is believed to have its roots in the ancient Chinese lion dance, which is still performed at New Year celebrations everywhere in the Chinese world. The lion dance was previously common also on many islands of Indonesia. Later, the Balinese lion figure acquired its own features, and became a creature combining various elements in a way typical only of Bali. Barong is not actually a lion, but a composite of various animals. The Barong types are named according to the dominating animal figure: Barong Asu combines the features of a dog and a lion, while Barong Machan resembles a tiger, the Barong Lembu has the shape of a cow, and the Barong Bankali has the features of a wild boar.

Grossly simplified, Barong is usually described as a manifestation of virtue. It is, however, too capricious and unpredictable to be interpreted unequivocally as such. Nevertheless, Barong is revered as the protector of villages, and its outfit and mask are regarded as sacred. During festivities, the Barong figure is carried around the village to the accompaniment of music. Each *banjar* or village council has at least one Barong mask and outfit of its own. The Barong figures are given human and identifiable traits. The history of many Barongs is known, particularly those regarded as exceptionally magical, and their reputation has spread throughout the island. On some occasions Barong is taken to a neighbouring village to meet his lover, and grand gatherings of many Barongs occasionally take place. In practice, the Barong processions, games, and gatherings are also a way for young men and women from neighbouring villages to become acquainted with one other.

Along with the various types of processions, specific forms of drama have evolved around Barong. Possibly the oldest of these is the hereditary *Barong Kedingkling,* a form of sacred dance-drama developed in the eighteenth century to ward off an epidemic. In this drama Barong appears together with monkey characters borrowed from the *Ramayana.* The performance lasts all day, beginning in the village temple and dispersing later throughout the village. The monkeys accompanying Barong are permitted various forms of mischief, such as pilfering food and well-meant teasing. Many villages have their own versions of this tradition. Barong is also a central figure in the *Calonarang* drama, and modern, non-ritual *Barong* dramas have been developed mainly for tourist shows.

Rangda is the other main mythological figure of the Balinese. Its symbolic significance is also complex and hard to interpret. It is often regarded as the incarnation of 'evil', but in fact the mask of this ferocious witch is revered in the village temples as a patron and a protector against evil. The mask has a horrifying appearance with its aggressive bulging eyes, long tusks, and red tongue extending down to the waist. Rangda is related to the Durga goddess of India, a ferocious emanation of the spouse of Shiva, the creator and destroyer—a kind of personification of holy wrath. Rangda is basically a manifestation of rage and destruction, and in performances many deities and supernatural beings often suddenly appear in the frightening shape of Rangda when experiencing such extreme moods.

Rangda, however, completely lacks the jocularity and good-naturedness of Barong. She is dangerous and destructive, possessing the power of making her opponents fall into a trance. The actor of the Rangda character may often himself fall into a trance while performing. The magical powers and destructiveness of Rangda place many requirements on the performer, who is often a respected individual in his community. Rangda's movements deliberately contradict all the ideals of Balinese classical dance. She often stands simply with her legs apart, trembling spasmodically, extending her hands, and shaking her long fingernails in readiness to attack her enemies. Like Barong, Rangda appears at village festivities, but she may also participate in large gatherings of Barongs and Rangdas as well as in many kinds of rituals and dramas.

The *Calonarang* is probably one of the best-known forms of drama, in which Barong and Rangda play central roles. It is an ancient East Javanese text in the Kawi language, and was originally influenced by Indian tantric teachings. It tells of a Javanese princess who controlled her spouse, a weak Balinese king, by means of black magic. In Bali the text was first converted into drama form in the 1890s, and it soon established its position as a central form of drama. According to Balinese custom, this new dance-drama employed existing histrionic conventions.

The various scenes of the original *Calonarang* drama are performed in the village temple and in various parts of the village, at road crossings, and in the cemetery. The two latter sites, like the sea-shore, are regarded by the Balinese as the most unholy and magically dangerous places in their environment. For the Balinese, black magic—the central theme of the *Calonarang* drama—is living reality, and some communities on the island still practise it. The *Calonarang* is a form of theatre laden with magical meaning, and was originally meant to ward off an epidemic. The plot is constructed as follows.

Calonarang, the widow of Girah (played by a male priest), a practitioner of black magic possessing two very powerful books, is furious because no one dares to marry her daughter. To avenge this wrong, the widow intends to destroy the kingdom with an epidemic brought about by black magic. She directs her pupils in a magic ritual (Plate 96). Young maidens with flowing hair and white costumes perform a strange dance, a kind of negative version of Balinese

96. Calonarang directs a magic ritual. (Photograph Sakari Viika)

classical dance. News of the widow's intentions has spread throughout the island, and the king decides to send his prime minister to fight the widow. The king instructs his minister, who then goes on with his retinue to meet the witch. The magical rite directed by the widow is approaching its climax when the prime minister arrives at the scene. The widow now appears in the shape of the furious Rangda, refusing to bow to the minister's demands. A battle is inevitable. Rangda falls into a trance and incites everyone to attack her.

The performance often reaches its culmination in the famous self-stabbing dance, where the villagers, incited to a blind rage, attack Rangda, who casts a spell over them with her white magic scarf. Finally, the villagers begin to stab themselves with their wavy-bladed krises (Colour Plate 37), as Rangda has the power to make people turn against themselves. This kris dance or *onying* was originally an independent form of trance ritual, but at present it is almost always performed at the end of a *Calonarang* or *Barong* performance. The village priests control the proceedings, moving the exhausted participants to the most sacred courtyard of the temple where they are revived with incense and holy water and brought back to consciousness. The *Calonarang* includes long comic scenes, where clowns, speaking in the vernacular, comment on the proceedings, entertaining the audience with their obscene humour. The Akademi Seni Tari Indonesia has created a shortened version of the *Calonarang*, from which the ritual elements have been excluded. The energetic and baroque characters of Barong and Rangda have particularly appealed to Western audiences. In the 1940s hotels began to stage shortened Barong and Rangda spectacles, which were the predecessors of the present tourist shows.

The Twentieth Century

The twentieth century brought an end to the isolated tranquillity of Bali. For centuries Balinese culture and theatre had been able to develop undisturbed. Now, influences flowed from all directions: from both the West and the island of Java. However, throughout their history, the Balinese have combined new ideas with old traditions, and foreign influences have stimulated Balinese theatre even in politically unstable times. The increasing mass tourism of recent years has created a new audience, which, however, has not always had a solely positive effect.

After the Dutch take-over of Bali in 1908, the traditional central court of Klungkung in Eastern Bali lost its former importance, and the focus of cultural life moved to North Bali near the Dutch colonial centre of Singaraja. New *gamelan* and dance clubs were established, and their competition led to a cultural renaissance in the 1910s–1930s. The most sensational novelty was a style of *gamelan* and dance called *kebyar*, which came about through a competition between two villages in creating musical and dance compositions.

With its wildly complex dynamics and its florid, embellished sound, the *kebyar* is probably the most expressive style of Balinese *gamelan*. In 1914 it was used to accompany the first performance of *kebyar* dance, the *kebyar legong*, performed by two maidens dressed as men. The new style became popular in only a few years. It was mainly developed by the legendary dancer I Nyoman Mario (Plate 97), who in 1925 presented the first performance of *kebyar duduk*, where the performer both dances and plays the *trompong*, an ancient percussion instrument placed in front of the *gamelan*.

Kebyar is an abstract non-narrative dance, where the performer interprets the rapidly changing moods of the *gamelan* with his or her movements and expressions. A characteristic feature of the style is that it is mostly performed in a crouching position, with the dancer often raising with one hand the hem of a narrow skirt resembling older *legong* costume. The dancer's bare arms trace expressive movements in the air while the hands and fingers are extended into delicate, quickly changing gestures. The dancer uses a fan to accentuate the rhythmic and emotional patterns of the *gamelan* accompaniment. Along with the costume, many movements and gestures also derive from *legong*. Several dance versions were developed at the height of the *kebyar* fever. The *Panji semirang* portrays the Princess Candra Kirana of the Panji tales disguised as a man—a typical feature of the *kebyar* intermixing male and female roles. The *kebyar bebancihan*, or neutral *kebyar*, is in turn a form of dance that can equally be performed by both men and women. Generally speaking, *kebyar* has had a decisive effect on the aesthetics of twentieth century Balinese dance.

I Nyoman Mario was greatly admired by both the Balinese and foreigners living on the island. Over the decades Westerners have had an increasing influence on the development of theatre and dance. Dutch colonial officials were in some cases patrons of the renaissance of North Balinese theatre, and the German-born painter and

97. I Nyoman Mario, the originator and exponent of *kebyar*. (*Theatre Arts Monthly*, August 1936; photograph Rose Covarrubias)

135

composer, Walter Spies, who settled in the small town of Ubud in Southern Bali, was in many ways instrumental in reshaping Balinese theatre. Spies was also the founder of the modern Balinese school of painting. He was visited by a wide range of Western artists and scholars from Charlie Chaplin to Margaret Mead, and he assisted European film-makers in planning the first documentary on Bali. For this film a new type of dance was created—the *cak* or *kecak*, which has found an established place in Balinese standard repertoire.

The *cak* (*kecak*) is based on the ancient dance chorus tradition. Men seated in the dark of night in circles around a large oil lamp chant the syllable 'cak-kecak-cak' with immense strength and astounding rhythmic precision (Plate 98). The fast abdominal breathing and the bursting vocal technique lead to hyperventilation and trance. Spies combined this archaic ritual tradition with a scene from the *Ramayana*, where Rama, Sita, and Ravana appear in the midst of the suggestive chorus to enact the scene where Sita is abducted. Sitting, singing, and dancing with their hands and upper torso, the chorus becomes the *Ramayana*'s army of monkeys. In the climax, the chorus, with heightened feverish pitch, rises as it takes part in the events of the drama. At present, *cak* (*kecak*) is frequently performed in many villages, but the shows are intended almost solely for tourists.

98. Ecstatic *cak* (*kecak*) dance; a modern Balinese painting. (Photograph author)

As the reputation of Bali spread throughout the world, Balinese dance troupes were invited to the West. In 1931 the first full group of Balinese dancers and musicians performed at the Colonial Exhibition in Paris, and in 1953 a Balinese group toured Europe and the United States. They were enthusiastically received, and their performances had a profound effect on many Western artists, including Antonin Artaud, who projected into Balinese performances his own concepts of 'total theatre' and 'Oriental dance'. In view of the Western audiences, I Nyoman Mario created for the tour a repertoire with short numbers, easily comprehended by foreigners, such as *Tambulilingan*, a composition portraying the mating of bumble-bees (Plate 99). Mario's choreographies have found an established position in Balinese dance repertoire.

When Indonesia achieved independence after a severe period of political strife, Bali became part of the new republic, and again after four hundred years of isolation Javanese influences increased in Balinese culture. In the field of dance, a new, nationalistic concept of art emerged, which was partly modelled after the socialist countries, and engendered a number of dances portraying the life of various

99. *Tambulilingan* depicting the dance of a bumble-bee; a composition by I Nyoman Mario. (Photograph Sakari Viika)

137

ethnic groups and social classes. These included the Peasants' Dance and the Weavers' Dance which reflected the ideas and aims of the new national government. In Bali the *kebyar* was chosen as the basic technique of these new, relatively simple dance compositions. The new ideas led to many experiments, which, however, did not achieve any permanent popularity. On the other hand, the *sendratari* dance-drama, created in the 1960s after Javanese models, shows no signs of diminishing popularity.

Sendratari (*seni*: drama; *tari*: dance) is a spectacular form of dance-drama, originally created in 1961 for the Prambanan Festival in Central Java to provide entertainment for both foreign and local tourists. Compared with other forms of classical dance-drama, it is more concise and more action-orientated, as the dialogue, recitation, and all ritual elements have been excluded. A narrator sitting in front of the *gamelan* presents the plot and the lines, while the dancers and large dancing choruses enact the story. *Sendratari* makes full use of Western stage techniques with coloured lights, spotlights, and other effects. Its overall dramaturgy mainly resembles Western narrative ballet. The subject of the original *sendratari* performed at the Prambanan Festival was the *Ramayana*. Soon after the first *sendratari* performance in Java, artists from the Balinese College of Performing Arts (KOKAR) staged for the first time a Balinese version of *sendratari* called *Jayaprana*, based on a popular love story— a kind of local 'Romeo and Juliet' tale.

In 1965 KOKAR presented the *Sendratari Ramayana*, a Balinese novelty based on the *Ramayana*, which became even more popular than *Jayaprana*, and many villages soon established their own *sendratari* groups. This genre combines elements of indigenous Balinese dance forms, such as *legong* and *kebyar* as well as Javanese dance traditions. The *sendratari* can be regarded as a kind of pan-Indonesian official state art, although in Bali the style has achieved an increasingly local flavour. Since the inauguration of the Bali Arts Festival in 1979, a large-scale *sendratari* spectacle has usually been the main event of the festival.

At present, Balinese theatre continues to be highly active. Despite new experiments traditional theatre has not lost any of its vitality. A favourite among the old forms is the *arja*, a kind of popular opera originally created in 1825 for the funeral of a Balinese prince. It was originally performed by an all-male cast, but in this century women replaced the male actors. The twentieth century has in many respects been a period of feminization in Balinese theatre; in many of the traditions, such as *sendratari*, female actors often play noble hero roles, while the practice of female impersonators has almost been forgotten. The all-female casting of *arja* is believed to have led to the predominance of vocal virtuosity, for at the same time the Balinese language has replaced the ancient Kawi court language. *Arja* became a true folk opera, popular all over the island. It is performed, in Balinese fashion, by dancing, and its main plot material is based on *The Adventures of Prince Panji*. Like other Balinese dance-dramas, it combines the most refined elements of dance and music with the earthiness and grotesque humour of clowns and servants. Along with village performances, *arja* can also be seen on television, but as the main emphasis is on vocal execution rather than physical enacting, the language barrier is more obvious to foreigners than in other forms of Balinese theatre.

While Bali has established its reputation as one of the world's best-known tourist paradises, its classical dance and theatre have become its true trade marks. Tourists and travellers come to Bali in large numbers, and every visitor usually attends one or two performances, while the more serious traveller may easily study Balinese dance in some of the numerous private schools operating on the island. This course of development has led to a number of essential changes. Previously, most performances were related to calendar feasts, but today they are held daily. The tastes, or assumed tastes, of tourists dictate the duration and structure of many performances. Most tourist shows consist of a potpourri of the main Balinese dance styles, often performed in a shortened and even somewhat simplified form. Even the annual Bali Arts Festival is basically an international event, and not the kind of traditional religious festivity that in earlier years provided the main theatrical performances.

In spite of reforms and mass tourism, there has also been serious work in Bali to maintain the old forms of theatre. The Akademi Seni Tari Indonesia and KOKAR institutes of dance and theatre, operating along pan-Indonesian lines, strive not only towards a new synthesis but also to study and revive old traditions. In the early 1970s cultural leaders decided that the most sacred *wali* dances must not be secularized or performed commercially for outsiders. This decision showed a clear concern for the dance and theatre traditions of the island, and their innermost sacral core. The dualism of the present situation may, however, explain the secret of the vitality of Balinese theatre. Throughout its long history, it has been susceptible to change, but its sacral core has remained unchanged. Bali will most probably remain one of the most interesting loci of Asian dance and theatre if Balinese theatre, while responding to the challenges of mass tourism, still retains its deep significance for the Balinese themselves.

6 Cambodia, Laos, and Malaysia

CAMBODIA, Laos, and Malaysia all have their own dance and drama traditions, although for various reasons actual performances are rather infrequent. Cambodia, the cradle of one of the most important dance traditions in the whole of South-East Asia, has in this century experienced political turmoil and continuous warfare. Consequently, it has not been possible to continue and maintain the grand court traditions. Laos, in turn, has more or less isolated itself, and it is difficult to obtain detailed information on present theatrical activities in the country. The Laotians had already adopted many of the Khmer traditions in the fourteenth century. These were also partly taken up by the Thais. Later, during the period of Thai domination, both Cambodia and Laos adopted Thai traditions, leading to the present relatively uniform style of dance and theatre throughout the whole region. This Thai-dominated tradition is partly shared by Malaysia, for the border provinces of both states have alternatively been under Thai or Malay rule. As a multiracial nation, Malaysia, however, has adopted dance and theatre traditions from elsewhere, but none of them can be regarded as a classical or national art form; they have mainly remained the heritage of specific ethnic groups threatened by Westernization and modern mass media.

Cambodia

The roots of Cambodian dance and theatre are believed to lie in ancient indigenous rituals, such as funerary ceremonies or rites connected to animistic or ancestor worship. Most of these predate the emergence of Funan (c.AD 100–500), the first Indianized kingdom in the present area of Cambodia. Early documentary sources clearly indicate strong Indian influences. One such source is a sixth-century inscription describing arrangements for the daily recitation of holy texts of Indian origin: the *Ramayana*, the *Mahabharata*, and the *Purana* texts. They were adopted from India together with the Sanskrit language and Hindu Brahmanism in its Shivaistic form, that is, with the god Shiva as its central manifestation. Numerous records from the sixth century onwards mention dance in connection with temple offerings performed by female dancers, who were donated or belonged to the temple as 'slaves of the god'. This was a common practice in India as well, where the temple dancers are known as *devadasi* ('slave of god').

140

The 'golden age' of Cambodian history was the Angkorean period from AD 802 to 1431, when splendid temples and cities such as the magnificent Angkor were built, and Khmer dance achieved the status of a kind of state art. Jayavarman II, the founder of the Khmer Empire came from Java in AD 802, and he is believed to have brought with him the early Javanese dance style—a strongly Indian-influenced dance tradition. According to visual sources—mainly the profuse and often magnificent temple reliefs where dance is abundantly depicted—the Indianized style soon merged with local traditions, resulting in the highly original Khmer dance style, which was to influence the development of dance in most parts of mainland South-East Asia. Dance had a prominent role in Khmer society. It was linked to the court, where the king dwelt surrounded by female dancers, and to the temples, where large female *corps de ballet* were responsible for ceremonial dance offerings. For example, over three thousand dancers are known to have been installed in the main state temples under the reign of Jayavarman VII.

Around this time, the *Ramker*, a Khmer version of the Indian *Ramayana* known as 'the jewel of Khmer literature', achieved a special position in Khmer culture in the same way as the later *Ramakien* in Thailand. Scenes from the epic are depicted in numerous temple reliefs, which give some kind of visual image of the Khmers' *Ramayana*-based dance-drama, assuming they had such a tradition (Figures 6–9).

Fig. 6
Dance of the aristocratic female characters in a relief at Angkor Wat. (Päivi Lempinen)

Fig. 7
Dynamic dance of an *apsara* or heavenly
nymph in a relief at Angkor Wat. (Päivi
Lempinen)

Fig. 8
Rama shooting the golden deer in a relief
at Angkor Wat. (Päivi Lempinen)

Fig. 9
Dance of a strong demon character in a
relief at Angkor Wat. (Päivi Lempinen)

The heyday of Khmer culture came to a sudden end in 1431, when Angkor was conquered by the Thais and the Khmer court and its artists were captured and brought to the Thai capital of Ayutthaya. The conquerors greatly valued the dance and theatre traditions of the Khmers and over the centuries they were adapted to Thai tastes and a Thai spirit. The result was what is known today as the classical style of Thai theatre and dance. Meanwhile, the powerless Khmer court was reduced to poverty, and during the ensuing centuries of insecurity it was constantly forced to change the site of its capital. This was naturally an unfavourable time for expensive court art, and the original Khmer traditions

100. A Khmer king in the early twentieth century wearing a strongly Thai-influenced court dress. (From *Länder och Folk i Ord och Bild*, Helsingfors: Holger Schildts Förlag, 1928)

gradually disappeared or were assimilated into the now Thai-dominated culture (Plate 100). Today's classical Khmer dance and theatre, therefore, derive mostly from Thailand, which repeatedly controlled the territory of present-day Cambodia, gradually establishing there its own art forms—themselves originally adopted from the Khmers. The transplanting of the Thai tradition was in many ways a total process, and in the nineteenth century, for example, two complete dance troupes were sent from the Thai court to the Khmer court. Until World War II the Royal Cambodian Ballet (Plates 101 and 102) performed its classical repertoire in the Thai language.

The Cambodian classical repertoire bears strong Thai influences. The rarely performed *lakhon khol* is basically a Khmer version of the Thai *khon*, a 'masked pantomime' depicting scenes from the *Ramayana* (Plate 103). *Nang shek thom*, or 'large hides', is one of the two types of Cambodian shadow theatre. Despite differences in the style of the puppets, it is closely related to the ancient *nang yai* shadow theatre of Thailand, and the forms of Cambodian dance-dramas called *roeung* were in turn strongly influenced by the *lakhon* dance-drama of Thailand.

The only classical dance troupe active in Cambodia is the Royal Cambodian Ballet, which until 1970 was supported by the Royal

101. The Royal Cambodian Ballet (*c*.1900).

Household at Phnom Penh under the name of *lakhon lueng* or 'the king's dancers'. In the twentieth century its repertoire has consisted of some 40 *roeung* dance-dramas and 60 pure dance numbers called *robam*, mostly group dances performed by women. The performances originally belonged to court rituals, but they are now aimed at general audiences, and innovations have been introduced to 'revive' the ancient Khmer dances. This has resulted in hybrid compositions combining the traditional Thai-based style with poses, costume, and jewellery copied from ancient Khmer reliefs (Colour Plate 38).

The classical traditions of Cambodia are to a great extent an integral part of the Indianized court culture of South-East Asia. On the other hand, *lakhon bassac*, the popular theatre of Cambodia, bears strong Vietnamese influences as a result of the close contacts between Cambodia and southern Vietnam during the period of French colonial rule. *Lakhon bassac* is a form of spoken theatre accompanied by Vietnamese/Chinese-influenced music which also uses a number of Thai–Khmer classical dance gestures. The stories are performed in the style of romantic comedy with additional farce elements. They mainly deal with mythical and historical themes from the *Jataka* stories, or were created in the spirit of these. French rule lasted for a century until World War II and had a clear influence

102. The Royal Cambodian Ballet (*c.*1900).

103. Cambodian court dancers performing *lakhon khol*. (From Raymond Cogniat, *Danses d'Indochine*, Paris: Éditions des Croniques du Jour, 1932)

on Cambodian theatre. The upper classes, familiar with French culture, experimented in drama in a French spirit, and these activities were sometimes supported by the ruler, Prince Sihanouk.

The history of Cambodian dance and drama still remains to be studied, and future research will no doubt bring forth a great deal of interesting information not only on developments within Cambodia but also on how much the Thai heritage of drama owes to the ancient Khmer tradition. The turmoil of the twentieth century makes it hard to assess the present state of Cambodian dance and drama. There is news of classical repertoire being revived, but also news of completely opposite developments. The Royal Cambodian Ballet, however, has been able to tour Europe and the United States, where the same theatrical heritage is maintained by active refugee troupes.

Laos

Laos received most of its classical dance and theatre traditions from its more powerful neighbours, first from the Khmers and later from the Thais. An indigenous feature is a reed organ called *khen*,

146

the national instrument of Laos, which is used to accompany a type of troubadour singing. This style is known as *mohlam*, and it developed from an old solo form into a duet, where male and female singers present love songs to a *khen* accompaniment. The *mohlam* or 'courts of love' folk songs are still extremely popular in Laos, and also among Lao speakers in neighbouring countries.

The Lao court at Luang Prabang is believed to have adopted its classical court culture from the Khmers in the mid-fourteenth century. This included the *Ramayana* epic, the Buddhist *Jataka* stories, as well as court dances. The small court was probably not able to afford large choruses of dancers, and the Khmer tradition was accordingly adapted to a smaller scale (Plate 104). After the Khmer Empire was conquered by the Thais, Laos split into three small kingdoms, which in the eighteenth and nineteenth centuries were ruled by the Burmese, Thais, Vietnamese, and Cambodians. Increasing Thai hegemony spread the Thai dance and drama tradition to Cambodia and Laos, and the rituals and entertainment of the tiny Lao courts were modelled along Thai lines (Plate 105). The repertoire of the Royal Lao Ballet mainly consisted of Thai-derived dances, often solo numbers or small group compositions performed solely by female dancers. Thailand was also the source of the most popular form of folk theatre, often called *mohlam*

104. Court scene, Laos. (From Raymond Cogniat, *Danses d'Indochine*, Paris: Éditions des Croniques du Jour, 1932)

147

105. Masked dancer from Luang Prabang, showing the strong Thai–Khmer influence in the repertoire of Lao theatre. (From Raymond Cogniat, *Danses d'Indochine*, Paris: Éditions des Croniques du Jour, 1932)

luong or 'story *mohlam*'. It came about in the early years of the twentieth century, when the Thai *likay* 'folk opera' was introduced into Laos. The *mohlam luong* performances originally followed the *likay* model, but in later years the thriving indigenous *mohlam* tradition began to dominate. The costumes and stories may still reflect Thai influences, but the music is clearly Lao art. In the 1980s Laos has partly isolated itself, and little is known about recent developments, for example, how the active role of Vietnam and the Soviet Union in the affairs of the country has affected the arts and cultural life in general.

148

Malaysia

Because of its geographical location, the Malay Peninsula has served as a kind of bridge between mainland and archipelagic South-East Asia. Malaysia combines a variety of ethnic and cultural elements: indigenous Malay, Javanese, Sumatran, Thai, Arab, Indian, Chinese, etc. Indianized court culture was adopted from Java and Sumatra, which dominated the Malay Peninsula before the emergence of the Islamic Sultanate of Malacca in the early fifteenth century. The ruling class of the sultanate had close ties with Islamic India, from where some of the sultans or their forefathers had arrived. Javanese influences continued to be felt, even during the period of Malaccan hegemony, as the sultan had huge retinues of Javanese workers and servants. The Sultanate of Malacca thus laid the basis not only for the Islamization of the peninsula but also for its ethnic diversity, which was gradually enriched by Chinese immigrants. The Portuguese conquered Malacca in 1511, heralding a long period of Western domination in the area of present-day Malaysia.

In this historical context it is only natural that the Malaysian theatrical tradition became eclectic. The various ethnic groups had their own drama traditions, none of which ever rose to the status of a national or classical form. The old Javanese influence can be traced in the *wayang Djava* and the *wayang Melayu*, two of Malaysia's three forms of shadow theatre. These genres differ mainly in the styles of their puppets. In *wayang Djava*, the puppets are highly stylized in the Javanese fashion, and both arms are movable. The *wayang Melayu* puppets, on the other hand, are less stylized with only one movable arm. The stories in both genres are mainly borrowed from the Javanese tradition, that is, the *Ramayana*, the *Mahabharata*, and the Prince Panji cycle. They are, however, all recited in the Malay language. Sometimes Islamic stories, such as the adventures of Amir Hamzah, are performed, and the new story material and a clear influence on the accompanying music are in fact the only evident contributions of Islam to the traditional theatre of Malaysia.

The third type of Malay shadow theatre, the *wayang Siam*, is linked to the culture of the Thais, Malaysia's northern Buddhist neighbours (Plate 106). The northern provinces of Malaysia were at times under Thai rule, and the population of the border areas has intermingled, and it is thus only natural that the Thai traditions of performing arts were established in these areas. The puppets of *wayang siam*, its performing technique, and the stories enacted all bear a close resemblance to the *nang talung* shadow theatre of South Thailand.

Thailand is also the source of the *Manora* (*lakhon nora*) dance-drama, which is still performed from time to time at state festivities. The *Manora* story is of general Asian provenance and has come to form part of the Buddhist *Jataka* collection. The dance style and

106. Figures from the Malaysian *wayang Siam* shadow theatre. (Photograph author)

costumes of its performances are direct loans from the Thai classical tradition.

The Malays are the largest individual ethnic group in modern-day Malaysia, but they have only a few drama traditions of their own. The most sophisticated, albeit rarely performed, one is the *mak yong*, an ancient form of court theatre from the state of Kelantan. In the twentieth century it has gradually developed into a folk form, usually performed by the wives of rice farmers in remote areas in Kelantan. The *mak yong* is believed to have been derived from ancient shamanistic healing rituals, and even today its performances are regarded as having magical significance and a special healing effect. Present-day *mak yong* combines indigenous rituals with elements borrowed from Indonesia, the Near East, and the *Manora* tradition of Thailand. It has a vast repertoire consisting mainly of dramatized folk-tales, where women play all the principal roles. The performances combine suggestive music and singing with dance and are staged under small bamboo roof structures open at the sides. They usually begin around 8 p.m. and continue until midnight, while a single play may take as many as five days to be completely enacted. Some of the smaller sultanate courts, from where the *mak yong* originated, still have their own *gamelan*-like musical traditions and court dances such as the solemn yet sensual *ayak-ayak* dance (Colour Plate 39), but performances are at present extremely rare, being mainly restricted to court festivities such as royal marriages or the sultan's birthday.

The popular theatre of the Malays is called *bangsawan* (*bangsa*: people; *wan*: noble). Its stories are from Arabian romances, other Islamic literature, and Malay history. They usually deal with rulers and aristocrats and some themes are borrowed from Western theatre. *Bangsawan* is a kind of melodramatic, semi-operatic drama combining songs with spoken theatre. Its popularity has faded, but it was extremely well-liked especially before World War II when *bangsawan* troupes toured as far as Sumatra and Java, influencing popular theatre there. The origins of *bangsawan* can be traced back to popular Indian theatre. In 1875 a Parsi theatre company from Bombay performed with great success in Penang, which led to the creation of *bangsawan*. The Indian minority in Malaysia cultivates to some degree their classical dance traditions, and the South Indian *bharatanatyam* solo dance, for example, is now taught and performed in Malaysia. The significant Chinese community, amounting to roughly one-third of the population, brought with them their thriving operatic tradition, which is discussed in detail in Chapter 7.

7 Chinese Theatre in South-East Asia

SOUTH-EAST ASIA is often described as the meeting-point of Indian and Chinese culture. As seen in the preceding chapters, Indian influences have been prominent in South-East Asia. Unlike the culture of India, the Chinese tradition was rarely assimilated into the local cultures. The Chinese element is, however, clearly evident in the demographic structure of these regions. Over the past seven centuries, millions of Chinese have moved to South-East Asia, bringing with them their own culture, which in most cases has survived as a type of minority culture. Accordingly, purely Chinese theatre genres live on in many South-East Asian countries. Over

107. Chinese opera scene; roof ornaments in a clan house in Penang, Malaysia. (Photograph author)

the centuries, the plots, general aesthetics, and performing techniques of Indian theatre became integral elements of South-East Asian traditions, while Chinese theatre has to a great degree preserved its original style. Chinese stories are performed by dancer-actors to the accompaniment of Chinese music, and the costumes and dance movements are also Chinese (Plate 107). The language of the performances is Chinese, and the audiences are mainly South-East Asian Chinese.

China and South-East Asia

China and South-East Asia have been in close contact for over two thousand years. Chinese annals mention South-East Asian kingdoms paying tribute and sending envoys to the emperor of China even before the present era. Direct Chinese influence was naturally strongest in the border regions. China ruled over large parts of present-day Vietnam for almost a thousand years, and Vietnamese culture adopted many Chinese elements. In other parts of South-East Asia, Chinese expansion was intermittent until the thirteenth century, and Chinese influences never had the same effect as Indian culture. The peak of Chinese political expansion was in the early stages of the Yuan dynasty (1279–1368), founded by the Mongols. In the 1280s the Mongols conquered an area extending from Hanoi to Pagan in present-day Burma. This had a great effect on political conditions in South-East Asia, but only a minor effect on the indigenous cultures.

Chinese culture was introduced into South-East Asia mainly through peaceful trade contacts and immigration. Chinese immigrants came for a variety of political and economic reasons. Those fleeing the invaders from the north often sought refuge in South-east China, which was traditionally a densely populated region. Along with increasing population pressure, the legendary riches of South-East Asia lured many Chinese to seek their fortunes there. Mass emigration was at first sporadic and dictated by political circumstances, but it increased with the consolidation of European colonial rule in South-East Asia and with the increased labour requirements of commerce and the mining industry. The end of the nineteenth century was the main period of emigration, when South-East Asia, the 'Eldorado of Asia' appealed to ever-increasing numbers of Chinese. Men were often the first to arrive, and many of them were assimilated into the local population through marriage. Later emigrants included women, which led to the formation of Chinese communities.

The immigrants came mainly from the coastal regions of South-east China—the provinces of Guangdong, Fujian, and Guangxi, and from the island of Hainan. On the South-East Asian mainland they mostly found their way into the regions of Cambodia, Cochin-China, Burma, and above all Thailand and Malaysia. In Thailand, where the Chinese had a long tradition even before this tide of mass immigration, the new arrivals were at first employed in rubber plantations and mines, and as village shopkeepers. Over the years, they came to dominate commerce and trade. Thailand became the home of speakers of the Hainan, Mei Hsien, and Chao Chu dialects of Chinese. In Buddhist Thailand the Chinese element assimilated with relative ease into the mainstream culture.

The Malay Peninsula, where the first Chinese had arrived in the fifteenth century, appealed to eighteenth- and nineteenth-century immigrants because of its large rubber plantations and the prospects of trade and commerce. When the British established ports on the island of Penang and in Singapore, a large Chinese work-force was required. The Chinese settled mostly in the towns, soon creating their own urban culture, which still thrives in George Town on Penang Island, in Malacca, and in Singapore, which broke away from Malaysia in 1965. The Chinese settlers of Malaysia and Singapore are mostly speakers of the Hokkien, Cantonese, Hakka, and Hainanese dialects. In the multiethnic society of Malaysia the Chinese are a prominent group, and Singapore is to a large degree a Chinese metropolis.

The Chinese population of Indonesia are mostly speakers of the Hakka, Chao Chu, and Teochew dialects. In the twentieth century, political strife in Indonesia has led the Chinese to abandon many of the visible expressions of their culture. Wherever the Chinese settled, they brought with them their own dialects, customs, and culture. Where possible, they built their dwellings, clan houses, and temples in the traditional manner of their provinces, or even in the specific styles of their native villages. South-East Asia thus became the new home of the South-east Chinese cultural heritage, which included a highly developed theatrical tradition.

The Development of Chinese 'Opera' Styles

Literary and visual sources offer a relatively large body of data on the early history of Chinese theatre. In China, as elsewhere, the roots of theatre lie in ancient rituals. Before Confucianism and Taoism evolved as systems of religious thought and philosophy (c.500–400 BC), shamanism was the main form of religion in China. In shamanistic rituals, the shaman-priest usually contacts spirits in a trance, acting as a mediator between his community and the spirit world. These rituals included many theatrical features, and they are believed to have been the basis from which Chinese theatre developed. In addition to rituals, performances of martial arts and acrobatics are known to have been held at a very early stage. When Chinese theatre later developed into its present forms, both acrobatics and the martial arts were assimilated as an essential part of its movement techniques.

Chinese culture flourished during the Tang dynasty (618–907), as international contacts via the Silk Route introduced music and theatre traditions from India and Central Asia. Ming Huang, the most famous ruler of this period, established at his palace the legendary Liyuan or Pear Garden theatre school. A number of drama texts of this period have been preserved, and many Tang literary themes are still found in the repertoire. Large-scale spectacles were staged in the court along with smaller dance and mime performances. This period also marked the creation of *canjunxi*, a form of theatre operating with comic stock characters.

In the Song dynasty (960–1279) Chinese theatre developed towards its present 'operatic' forms, and the division into northern and southern opera styles came into being. The Western term 'opera' is apt from our perspective, as the actors themselves sing their dialogue. This is not very common in Asia, and in many Indian and South-East Asian traditions the players enact the plot with their gestures, expressions, and dance-like gestures, while off-stage narrators and musicians recite and sing the dialogue. Despite apparent similarities, there are many differences between Western and Chinese opera. In China not only the vocal parts but all the histrionic elements are dictated by the musical accompaniment. The actors often accentuate their dialogue and 'arias' with highly conventionalized facial expressions and dance-like movements. Chinese opera has in fact assimilated a great number of ancient dance traditions, which have long since ceased to be observed.

The Yuan dynasty (1280–1368) was the period of Mongol rule in China, but it has also been called the golden age of Chinese drama. Former officials and scholars, who fled foreign rule to Southern China, concentrated their literary efforts on drama and other arts. They created the so-called Yuan plays, which are still regarded as the classics. A wall-painting fragment from the Yuan period portrays a company of actors, and shows that in Yuan drama historical costumes were worn, as in most forms of Chinese opera even today. Role categories and facial make-up also resembled present-day Chinese opera. Some of the lines are known to have been sung, but not much else is known about the musical tradition of Yuan drama.

Kunqu is the oldest Chinese opera style that is still being performed. It was created around the middle of the Ming dynasty (1368–1644). With its flowing melodies, it is a typically southern style of opera. *Kunqu* was the joint creation of musicians, actors, and authors, and it soon became established as an art form of the court and the intellectuals. *Kunqu* drama is on a high literary level, and modern-day audiences find it extremely hard to understand its complex language. In *kunqu*, the singing actors perform in gentle legato-like dance movements, and the vocal parts, accentuated with trills, are accompanied by a soft-sounding bamboo flute, also a typical feature of South Chinese opera. *Kunqu* became very popular among the upper classes, developing into two main types: *nankun* in the south and *beikun* in the north. In later years the northern style adopted elements of Peking opera, which in the eighteenth century achieved the former status of *kunqu* as a nation-wide, court-sponsored style of theatre.

During the Qing dynasty (1644–1911) the Manchus ruled China from Beijing, and the southern *kunqu* opera gradually waned in popularity. Emperor Qianlong, a fervent patron of the arts, invited performers of various local operas to his capital, which led to the creation of a new opera style. By combining different traditions, a group of artists developed a new style called *jingju*, the opera of the capital. In the West and gradually elsewhere it has come to be called Beijing or Peking opera.

Peking opera is a typically northern style, where the singer's voice is supported by a high-pitched violin-like instrument, while the orchestra includes a rich and precisely accentuated percussion section. Like other Chinese styles of opera, Peking opera is also a theatre of stock characters. Each role type has its own standard costume, facial make-up, and voice register, all based on historical models. The various roles also have their own techniques of movement. The main *dan* or female role is that of a noble heroine, singing in a piercingly high register in a falsetto-like voice. This derives from earlier times, when male or eunuch actors played female parts. The heroine moves in a slightly wavy manner with tiny feminine steps, and all of her movements and gestures express feminine grace. The *hua dan* is a wanton woman, or type of soubrette character, who adds to her basic gracefulness a touch of flirtatiousness, and sometimes even vulgarity.

The main *sheng* or male role is that of a noble hero, 'a young scholar', singing in a high register. His technique of movement reflects overall charm and cultivation. The *chou* or clown roles are a separate group, which can be recognized by the white make-up around their noses. The *jing* or painted-faced characters are baroque figures, often wearing high-soled cothurnus. The *jing* have facial make-up of bright, glowing colours, which the initiated viewer can interpret as revealing the characters' psychological qualities. The painted-faced *jing* move in an exaggeratedly bombastic way. In stepping forward, the forbidding figure of a general may raise his foot to ear-level, while the movements of arms and body are strongly articulated.

Older Yuan drama and *kunqu* repertoire may be used as plot material in Peking opera. Popular librettos are also derived from novels such as *Sanguo zhi yanyi* (The Romance of the Three Kingdoms) or *Honglou men* (The Dream of the Red Chamber). The operas fall into two main categories: *civil plays* of human relations and often love stories; and *military plays* dealing with historical battles and political intrigues. The latter often include acrobatic martial scenes with magnificently dynamic action, stunning the audience with their speed and demanding technique.

There are many types of opera in China. The rarely performed *kunqu* and the still popular Peking opera are known everywhere as kinds of national styles. As the Chinese language is tonal, its countless dialects have created their own distinctive stock melodies.

In almost all parts of China the characteristic dialects and their respective melodies have led to minor local opera traditions, which, however, all share a common plot material and conceptions of histrionics and aesthetics. Peking opera remains the most popular of the some 300 opera styles being performed in the People's Republic of China.

Forms of Chinese Theatre in South-East Asia

It is not known when Chinese theatre or 'opera' first found its way into South-East Asia. Chinese musical instruments were, however, adopted in the local traditions of the mainland regions after the Mongol invasions. In Thailand, Cambodia, and especially Vietnam, Chinese stories were adapted and are still being used in certain forms of popular theatre. The first Western reference to Chinese opera in South-East Asia is most probably an account of a 'detestable' Chinese performance seen in the late seventeenth century by the Abbé de Choisy on a visit to the Thai capital of Ayutthaya. Ayutthaya was at the time a highly international metropolis with its own sections for Western and Chinese inhabitants. By the Ayutthaya period, the local Chinese had established their position in Thai society. Chinese opera has

108. Chinese opera staged in Thailand; an early nineteenth-century wall painting at Wat Phra Keo, Bangkok. (Photograph author)

probably been performed for centuries in Thailand (Plate 108) and in the old Chinese centres of the Malay Peninsula. Over the centuries, Chinese opera became more and more established along with the growth of the Chinese colonies in South-East Asia.

The immigrants brought with them the local opera types of their home regions. The old, sophisticated *kunqu* of South China and its northern successor, *jingju* (Peking opera) were—and still are—almost unknown in South-East Asia. The most popular opera form in Thailand is Teochew, while in Malaysia most contemporary opera groups have specialized in Canton opera. Other dialect groups have their own opera companies. In Singapore, the majority of the troupes are Hokkien Chinese.

In practice, the outward differences of these subgenres have become obscured. For example, costumes and facial make-up have become uniform, and a viewer unfamiliar with the dialects cannot distinguish between different genres. A common feature of South-East Asian Chinese theatre is the prominent role of female actors. In *jingju*, for example, men have traditionally played the female parts, and women were not allowed on the stage until the 1920s. In Southern China, on the other hand, women have traditionally played female, and sometimes even male parts, a practice adopted by most of the Chinese theatrical traditions of South-East Asia. Acrobatic scenes, so typical of the northern *jingju* tradition, are rare in South-East Asia.

In Mainland China opera was cultivated in impressive court theatres, on the private stages of the merchant élite, and in the tea-rooms of the ordinary, paying public. As there were no Chinese courts in South-East Asia, Chinese theatre was mainly aimed at an audience of ordinary workers. Before the breakthrough of cinema in the first decades of the twentieth century, permanently established Chinese opera houses, operating on a commercial basis, drew full houses night after night. In addition to many opera houses, Singapore also had opera stages in its large amusement parks. The period of the large opera houses came to an end after World War II, when cinema grew in popularity, and at present, almost all commercial opera troupes in South-East Asia are touring companies.

At present, approximately a hundred professional Chinese theatre companies are operating in Thailand, Malaysia, and Singapore. Their main clients are clan organizations and temple committees, which commission performances for religious festivities. The main events are the birthday celebrations of various deities and the Festival of Hungry Ghosts, which normally falls in the months of August or September. Many Chinese temples in South-East Asia have their own permanent stages for opera performances. Impressive old stages are to be found, for example, in the temple of Cheng Hoong Teng in Malacca (Plate 109) and in the clan house of the Khoo family in Penang. Touring companies, however, usually perform in public squares or on temporary

109. Chinese opera stage; Cheng Hoong Teng temple, Malacca. (Photograph author)

stages erected in temple courtyards. The bamboo and wooden structures are covered with colourful backdrops, and above the stage is a banner with the name of the troupe. Performances may last all day, although in the morning and around noon there may not be an audience, as the performances are primarily intended for deities or the spirits of ancestors.

In Thailand, however, Chinese opera is often performed at Thai temple festivals. These performances are sponsored by Chinese religious committees, which also select the repertoire. This is an old tradition; early nineteenth-century wall paintings in the Temple of Wat Phra Keo in Bangkok depict festivities where Chinese opera was performed alongside various forms of Thai theatre.

When interest in opera was at its peak in the 1920s and 1930s, star actors earned sums of money in one night that can well be compared to the fees of modern-day film stars. Opera waned in popularity after the spread of cinema, and many opera houses were converted into movie theatres. The fees paid to performers have remained almost the same over the decades. However, Chinese opera in South-East Asia is hardly in danger of extinction, as religious festivals still provide regular commissions. Many groups perform outside the borders of their own countries. Thai opera companies, for example, often visit Malaysia, and visiting opera companies from Hong Kong and South China provide added attractions to the audiences of Chinese theatre (Plate 110).

159

110. Visiting guest star from Hong Kong performing in a Chinese opera house in Bangkok. (Photograph author)

Amateur performances also play an important role. In Singapore, for instance, the state supports several opera societies, and high-quality amateur opera can be seen on even the principal stages of the city.

In addition to opera, the Chinese introduced their own traditions of shadow and puppet theatre. In Malaysia glove or finger puppet performances are a common feature of temple festivals (Plate 111), and the impressive collections of Chinese puppets in the National Museum in Bangkok bear witness to the popularity of Chinese puppet theatre in Thailand. In Java, on the other hand, *wayang Cina*, a local combination of Chinese and Javanese shadow theatre, evolved, with Chinese stories being performed with predominantly Javanese-type shadow puppets (Plate 112). It is a rare example of a blend of local and Chinese traditions. Similarly, the famous Barong character of Balinese theatre is believed to have been influenced by the Chinese lion dance, traditionally performed in New Year celebrations. In other respects, Chinese and indigenous traditions of theatre have become mixed only in the immediate vicinity of the Chinese cultural sphere, for example, in Cambodia. Here, an indigenous form of local theatre, the *lakhon bassac,* developed in the nineteenth and twentieth centuries. In its music and movements, *lakhon bassac* combines both local and Chinese elements. Cambodia received Chinese influences via Vietnam, where the theatrical traditions were strongly influenced by its great northern neighbour.

160

111. Chinese glove puppet theatre
     performed in Penang. (Photograph
     author)

112. Puppets of *wayang Cina*, the
     shadow theatre of the Chinese
     minority of Java. (Photograph
     author)

8 Vietnam

VIETNAM is the only South-East Asian country where the Chinese tradition predominates in theatre and dance. This is the result of various historical and geographical factors. Geographically, Vietnam belongs to both East and South-East Asia. The Indo-Chinese Peninsula—of which Vietnam occupies a narrow stretch in its eastern half—is essentially a southern extension of the Chinese land mass. It is thus only natural that the political power and cultural influence of China have been present throughout Vietnam's history. Even early archaeological finds show Chinese influence, which spread to the original territory of the Vietnamese in Tonkin and northern Annam at least two centuries before the present era. By 40 BC, these regions were incorporated into the Chinese Empire, to which they belonged for the following nine centuries.

In other parts of South-East Asia, religions, the language of the court, mythology, law, and art were all adopted from India. The Vietnamese, on the other hand, received the cornerstones of their culture from China, viz. Confucianism, Taoism, Chinese Buddhism, the language of the ruling class, the Chinese classics, the civil service examination system, and their whole model of administration. Indian influences, prominent elsewhere, were adopted via the Indianized kingdom of Champa, conquered by the Vietnamese around the fifteenth century. With increasing Chinese domination, however, Indianized elements were to remain marginal in Vietnamese culture.

The Vietnamese have often fought for their independence. The first, short-lived, Vietnamese dynasty was established around the middle of the tenth century, and over the centuries, the Vietnamese gained control over areas in Annam and further south in Cochin-China, the traditional territory of the Khmers. The division between North and South Vietnam is geographical: the coastal stretch is long and narrow, and civilization concentrated around two river valleys, the Red River in the north and the Mekong in the south. Central Vietnam, however, has a distinct identity as a mountainous region. Cochin-China was for a long time the European name for the whole of Vietnam, but from the end of the eighteenth century the French used it only in referring to the south. They called the northern parts Tonkin and the centre Annam, although the latter term was sometimes used for the country as a whole. The Vietnamese never used these terms; for them, the south was Nam Bo, the centre Trung Bo, and the north Bac Bo. The history of Vietnam can be broadly divided into three cultural periods:

1. tenth to fourteenth century: joint influence of Chinese and Indian culture;
2. fifteenth to eighteenth century: predominantly Chinese influence; and
3. eighteenth century: period of Western influence.

Vietnamese history is marked by a continuous struggle against Chinese hegemony and conflicts with other conquering powers, such as the Khmer Empire and the Thais. In 1802 a new state of Vietnam was formed with its capital in Hué, where the court maintained its own Chinese-influenced traditions of art and culture. The court and its customs lived on even after 1857, when French military rule was established. In 1887 the territory of Vietnam that became part of a new French Indo-Chinese Union, which after 1893 included Cambodia and Laos, was ruled by a French governor-general residing in Hanoi. The court in Hué relinquished the remnants of its former political power after World War II, shortly before Ho Chi Minh declared the founding of the Democratic People's Republic of Vietnam in September 1945. The tragic war in Vietnam, which began in the 1960s, and its various consequences have left their mark on the country, but much of its traditional, and particularly popular, culture has been preserved to the present day.

In this historical context, it is only natural that Chinese influence is prominent in Vietnamese theatrical traditions. According to oral tradition, a Vietnamese ruler of the early eleventh century employed a Chinese actor to teach his court actors the art of 'Chinese satirical theatre'. It is not known, however, what was exactly meant by 'satirical theatre'. At the time of the Mongol invasion in the late thirteenth century, the Vietnamese adopted Chinese 'opera'. It is known that Vietnamese soldiers captured a Chinese opera troupe, and some of the imprisoned actors were employed to teach their art to the local actors.

The Chinese opera style was thus adopted by the Vietnamese at an early stage. Vietnamese court opera is called *hat boi* (*hat*: to sing; *boi*: gesture, pose), which developed into its classical form in the fourteenth century (Plate 113). Outwardly, it resembles Chinese opera to a great degree. As in Chinese opera, the *hat boi* actors sing their lines and employ dance-like gestures. The histrionic conventions were also adopted from China, but the music, despite various Chinese influences, represents indigenous tradition. At first, Chinese classics provided material for the plots, but later librettos relating to Vietnamese history were also written, and Chinese stories and tales were adapted to local tastes and conditions. Significant librettists were Dao Duy Tu (1572–1634) and Dao Tan (1848–1908).

Hat boi gradually became popular throughout the country, especially in the south. Chinese influence continued over the centuries,

113. Battle scene from a Vietnamese court opera. (From Dr Georg Buschan, *Die Sitten der Völker*, Stuttgart, Berlin, Leipzig: Union Deutsche Verlagsgesellschaft, SA)

and *hat boi* closely followed the development of many Chinese opera styles in their various phases. Facial make-up, for instance, is based on eighteenth-century Chinese standards (Colour Plate 40). The troupes originally performed for the court and the nobility in palaces and private apartments, but at the beginning of the nineteenth century a permanent opera stage was built at the imperial palace in Hué. The court had extravagant tastes in opera, and official records mention that Emperor Tu Duc (1848–83) employed an opera troupe of 150 female actors in his court as well as a renowned Chinese opera star. The emperors at the court of Hué preserved the *hat boi* tradition until 1945, but with the end of imperial patronage, this tradition soon degenerated, and at present most commercial performances of *hat boi* are only distant echoes of the classical court opera.

Along with *hat boi*, the court also developed ceremonial dances imitating the practice of the Chinese imperial court (Plates 114 and 115). In other parts of South-East Asia the poses and hand gestures of almost all the main forms of court dance reflect a more or less direct Indian influence, whereas Vietnamese court dances, in their slow ceremoniality, echo ancient Chinese prototypes. Dances were often accompanied by large instrumental ensembles. The main dance types included the so-called dances of fabulous animals,

164

114. Chinese-influenced Vietnamese ceremonial court dance. (From Raymond Cogniat, *Danses d'Indochine*, Paris: Éditions des Croniques du Jour, 1932)

which included mythical beings such as the unicorn and the phoenix. The largest dance ceremonies included the civilian dance *van vu* and the military dance *va vu*, which were still performed in this century at the Sacrifice to Heaven and Earth, an important state ritual which was adopted from China. These ceremonial dances were performed by two *corps de ballet*, each consisting of 64 dancers arranged in eight rows. In the early years of the twentieth century the original repertoire of court dance was reduced, and the tradition of court dance appears to have died out when royal patronage ended.

Court opera had a great effect on the creation of *cai luong*, Vietnam's main form of popular theatre. In the 1920s *cai luong* developed from a type of musical interlude into a specific form of drama. The strict stylistic conventions of *hat boi* were relaxed, and the musical accompaniment of *cai luong* consists mainly of beautiful South Vietnamese melodies. One of the most popular stock melodies is a heart-rending love lament called *vong co*, written in the 1920s by Cao Van Lau, which can still be heard several times in every *cai luong* performance. Plots can still be based on tales adapted from *hat boi* repertoire, but *cai luong* performances often depict Vietnamese history or more timely topics. The *hat boi* court opera was usually performed in front of a single backdrop

115. A variant of the Vietnamese ceremonial court dance. (From Raymond Cogniat, *Danses d'Indochine*, Paris: Éditions des Croniques du Jour, 1932)

with only a table and a couple of chairs as props, as in Chinese classical opera. *Cai luong*, on the other hand, attempts to create an illusionistic stage setting with changing backdrops, as in Western theatre, while the basic costumes follow the customs of South Chinese opera. Along with these semi-historical fantasy costumes, modern dress can be used according to the theme of the performance. Melodramatic elements and sensational stage effects are typical of this form of popular theatre. Unlike other countries in South-East Asia, Vietnam developed a form of spoken theatre, the *kich*, which was inspired by French models.

Vietnam also has its own tradition of puppet theatre. During French rule a Western-influenced type of marionette theatre was introduced in South Vietnam. In North Vietnam, an old and very rare form of puppet theatre has survived, and has even been revived in the 1980s. In a number of small villages near Hanoi, water puppet theatre is still performed at certain festivities, as it has been in times past. The puppeteers, usually ordinary villagers, manipulate 30- to 40-centimetre-high puppets while standing in water. The performance is usually arranged at the village ponds, typical features of Vietnamese villages. A temporary structure is constructed above the water, from which a bamboo curtain is

166

hung to shield the puppeteers from the audience sitting on the banks of the pond (only one permanent stone structure is known to exist). The puppets are manipulated with rods hidden under the water, while a small orchestra accompanies the narrators who recite the story and the necessary lines.

The repertoire, varying from village to village, consists of standard scenes, partly dealing with Vietnamese history, classics, and domestic affairs. A performance usually begins with a show of fireworks, after which Teu, the stock clown, makes his entrance, being followed by special animal scenes in which horses, frogs, turtles, etc. are introduced. Ploughing with water-buffaloes, fishing scenes, and other everyday activities are also enacted (Plates 116 and 117). The most dramatic scenes are those of Vietnamese history, such as famous sea battles. It was formerly believed that water puppet theatre came to Vietnam from China, where early literary references to this art form exist. At present, experts believe that

116. Ploughing with water-buffaloes; Vietnamese water puppet theatre. (Photograph Satu Aaltonen)

117. Crossing the water with the dragon boat; Vietnamese water puppet theatre. (Photograph Satu Aaltonen)

the Chinese adopted water puppetry from the Vietnamese. This view is supported by the fact that the Chinese term for water puppetry appears to be derived from the Vietnamese name. In the 1970s, water puppetry performances were organized in only a few villages, but partly because of the interest of the foreign community in Hanoi, a project was launched by Western countries and cultural institutes to document and propagate this unique tradition. In later years, commercial performances have been held in Hanoi, and water puppet troupes have toured abroad.

Bibliography

General

Asian Puppets, The Wall of the World, Los Angeles: University of California, 1976.

Bowers, Faubion, *The Drama in the East: A Survey of Asian Dance and Drama*, New York: Grove Press, 1956.

Brandon, James R., *Brandon's Guide to Theater in Asia*, Honolulu: University Press of Hawaii, 1976.

————, *Theatre in Southeast Asia*, Cambridge: Harvard University Press, 1967.

———— (ed.), *The Performing Arts in Asia*, Paris: UNESCO, 1971.

Cogniat, Raymond, *Danses d'Indochine*, Paris: Éditions des Croniques du Jour, 1932.

Hall, D. G. E., *A History of South-East Asia*, 4th edn., London and Basingstoke: Macmillan, 1981.

Kindermann, Heinz (ed.), *Fernöstliches Theater*, Stuttgart: Alfred Kröner Verlag, 1966.

Leims, Thomas (ed.), '... *Ich Werde deinen Schatten essen', Das Theater des Fernen Ostens*, Berlin: Akademie der Kunste, 1985.

Mackerras, Colin, *Chinese Drama: A Historical Survey*, Beijing: New World Press, 1990.

The Natya Sastra of Bharatamuni, translated by Board of Scholars, Raga Nrtya Series No. 2, Delhi: Sri Satguru Publications, SA, n.d.

Purcell, Victor, *The Chinese in South-East Asia*, 1st edn., 1951; 2nd edn., Kuala Lumpur: Oxford University Press, 1965.

Vatsyayan, Kapila, *Indian Classical Dances*, New Delhi: Publication Division, Ministry of Information and Broadcasting, 1974.

Burma

Pe Hla (ed. and tr.), *Konmara Pya Zat, an Example of Popular Burmese Drama in the XIX Century by U Pok Ni*, Vol. I, London: Luzac, 1952.

Maung Htin Aung, *Burmese Drama: A Study, with Translations, of Burmese Plays*, Calcutta: Oxford University Press, 1937.

Sein, Kenneth (Maung Khe) and White, J. A., *The Great Po Sein, A Chronicle of the Burmese Theatre*, Bloomington: Indiana University Press, 1965.

Cambodia

Cravath, Paul, 'The Ritual Origins of the Classical Dance Drama of Cambodia', *Asian Theatre Journal*, Vol. 3, No. 2 (1986), pp. 179–203.

Indonesia

Bandem, I Madé and deBoer, Frederik Eugene, *Kaja and Kelod: Balinese Dance in Transition*, Singapore: Oxford University Press, 1981.

Brandon, James R., *On Thrones of Gold: Three Javanese Shadow Plays*, Cambridge: Harvard University Press, 1970.

Buurman, Peter, *Wayang Golek: The Entrancing World of Classical Javanese Puppet Theatre*, Singapore: Oxford University Press, 1988.

Covarrubias, Miguel, *Island of Bali*, New York: Knopf, 1937; reprinted Singapore: Oxford University Press, 1972.

van Groenendael, Victoria M. Clara, *Wayang Theatre in Indonesia: An Annoted Bibliography*, Koninklijk Instituut voor Taal-, Land- en Volkenkunde, Bibliographical Series 16, Leiden: Koninklijk Instituut voor Taal-, Land- en Volkenkunde, 1987.

Holt, Claire, *Art in Indonesia*, Ithaca: Cornell University Press, 1967.

Mulyono, Sri, *Human Character in the Wayang*, Singapore: Gunung Agung, 1981.

Van Ness, Edward C. and Prawirohardjo, Shita, *Javanese Wayang Kulit: An Introducion*, Singapore: Oxford University Press, 1979.

Ramseyer, Urs, *The Art and Culture of Bali*, Oxford: Oxford University Press, 1977.

Rebling, Eberhard, *Die Tanzkunst Indonesiens*, Berlin: Henschelverlag Kunst und Gesellschaft, 1989.

Soedarsono, *Dances of Indonesia*, Jakarta: Gunung Agung, 1974.

———, *Wayang Wong: The State Ritual Dance Drama in the Court of Yogyakarta*, Yogyakarta: Gadjah Mada University, 1984.

de Zoete, Beryl and Spies, Walter, *Dance and Drama in Bali*, London: Faber & Faber, 1938; reprinted Singapore: Oxford University Press, 1973.

Malaysia

Gunawardana, A. J., 'Theatre in Malaysia: An Interview with Mustapha Kamil Yassin' *Drama Review*, Vol. 15, No. 3 (1971), pp. 102–7.

Malm, William P., 'Malaysian Ma'yong Theatre', *Drama Review*, Vol. 15, No. 3 (1971), pp. 108–14.

Sweeney, Amin, *Malay Shadow Puppets, the Wayang Siam of Kelantan*, London: Trustees of British Museum, 1972.

Singapore

Vente, Ines, *Wayang: Chinese Street Opera in Singapore*, Singapore: MPH Bookstores, 1984.

Thailand

HH Prince Dhaninivat Kromamun Bidyalabh Bridhyakorn, *Shadow Play (The Nang)*, Thai Culture, New Series No. 3, 5th edn., Bangkok: Fine Arts Department of Thailand, 1973.

HH Prince Dhaninivat Kromamun Bidyalabh Bridhyakorn and Danith Yupho, *The Khon*, Thai Culture, New Series No. 6, 5th edn., Bangkok: Fine Arts Department of Thailand, 1973.

Danith Yupho, *The Khon and Lakon: Dance Dramas Presented by the*

Department of Fine Arts, Bangkok: Fine Arts Department of Thailand, 1963.

———, *Khon Masks*, Thai Culture, New Series No. 7, 4th edn., Bangkok: Fine Arts Department of Thailand, 1971.

———, *The Preliminary Course of Training in Thai Theatrical Art*, Thailand Culture, New Series No. 13, 7th edn., Bangkok: Fine Arts Department of Thailand, 1980.

Ingersoll, Fern S. (translation and introduction), *Sang Thong: A Dance Drama from Thailand, Written by King Rama II and the Poets of His Court*, Rutland and Tokyo: Charles E. Tuttle Company, 1973.

Rutnin, Mattani (ed.), *The Siamese Theatre: A Collection of Reprints from the Journals of the Siam Society*, Bangkok: Siam Society, 1975.

Vietnam

Song Ban, *The Vietnamese Theatre*, Hanoi: Foreign Languages Publishing House, 1960.

Than Van Khe, *Marionettes sur eau du Vietnam*, Paris: Maison des Cultures du Monde, 1984.

Index

Numbers in italics refer to Colour Plates.